Making Sense of

WINE TASTING

Your Essential Guide to Enjoying Wine
Fifth Edition

Alan Young

Making Sense of

WINE TASTING

Your Essential Guide to Enjoying Wine

Fifth Edition

Alan Young

Wine Appreciation Guild
South San Francisco, California

OTHER BOOKS BY ALAN YOUNG

An Encounter With Wine
(Wine Information Bureau, Perth 1977, new edition 1986)

Australian Wines and Wineries
(Horwitz Grahame, Sydney 1983)

Australia-New Zealand Wine Year Book
(International Wine Academy, 1986)

Making Sense of Wine—A Study in Sensory Perception
(Greenhouse Publications, Melbourne, 1986, new editions 1989, 1995)

Making Sense of Wine Tasting
(Lennard Books, London, 1987)

CHARDONNAY—The Definitive Guide
(Sidgwick & Jackson, London, 1988, new edition 1989)

CHARDONNAY—Your International Guide
(International Wine Academy, San Francisco, 1991, new edition 1994)

I.W.A. Study Manuals #1 & 2
(International Wine Academy, San Francisco, 1992)

Wine is Fun!
(International Wine Academy, San Francisco, 1995, Chinese edition 1997)

Wine Routes of Argentina
(International Wine Academy, San Francisco, 1999)

Wine Routes of Catalonia & Penedes
(International Wine Academy, San Francisco, 2001)

Pinot Noir—The Ultimate Enigma—In production

VIDEOS BY ALAN YOUNG

About Corks

Barrels, Casks & Coopers

Introduction to Viticulture

Introduction to Wine Making

Lodi Living

Making Sense of Wine

Murray—Mallee and the Outback

OTHER BOOKS BY THE WINE APPRECIATION GUILD
"The Best Wine Publisher in the US."
—Edward Cointreau, Gourmand World Cookbook Award

Africa Uncorked, John and Erica Platter (ISBN 1-891267-52-3)

Armagnac, Charles Neal (ISBN 1-891267-20-5)

The Bartender's Black Book, 9th ed. Stephen Kittredge Cunningham (ISBN 1-934259-17-9)

Benefits of Moderate Drinking, Gene Ford (ISBN 0-932664-60-1)

Biodynamic Wine Demystified, Nicholas Joly (ISBN 978-1-934259-02-3)

California Brandy Drinks, Malcom R. Hebert (ISBN 0-932664-21-0)

California Wine Drinks, William I. Kaufman (ISBN 0-932664-19-9)

Champagne & Sparkling Wine Guide, Tom Stevenson (ISBN 1-891267-41-8)

The Champagne Cookbook, Malcolm R. Herbert (ISBN 1-891267-70-1)

Cheese, Gabriella Ganugi (ISBN 1-891267-69-8)

Chile the Art of Wine, Sara Matthews (ISBN 1-891267-73-7)

Chilean Wine Heritage, Rodrigo Alvarado (ISBN 1-891267-80-9)

Chow! Venice, Shannon Essa and Ruth Edenbaum (ISBN 1-934259-00-4)

The Commonsense Book of Wine, Leon D. Adams (ISBN 0-932664-76-8)

Concepts in Wine Chemistry, Yair Margalit (ISBN 1-891267-74-4)

Concepts in Wine Technology, Yair Margalit (ISBN 1-891267-51-5)

Desert Island Wine, Miles Lambert-Gocs (ISBN 978-1934259-01-6)

Encyclopedia of American Wine, William I. Kaurman (ISBN 0-932664-39-3)

Epicurean Recipes of California Winemakers, Malcom Hebert (ISBN 0-932664-00-8)

Essential Guide to South African Wine, Elmari Swart (ISBN 062035500x)

Favorite Recipes of California Winemakers, (ISBN 0-932664-03-2)

Fine Wine in Food, Patricia Ballard (ISBN 0-932664-56-3)

Food & Wine Lovers' Guide to Portugal, Metcalfe and McWhirter (ISBN 095-57069-0-4)

The French Paradox, Gene Ford (ISBN 0-932664-81-4)

Ghost Wineries of the Napa Valley, Irene Whitford Haynes (ISBN 0-932664-90-3)

The Global Encyclopedia of Wine, Edited by Peter Forrestal (ISBN 1-891267-38-8)

Good Wine, Bad Language, Great Vineyards: Australia (ISBN 0977514722)

Good Wine, Bad Language, Great Vineyards: New Zealand (ISBN 0977514722)

Grands Crus of Bordeaux, Hans Walraven (ISBN 0-932664-94-6)

Grape Man of Texas, McLeRoy and Renfro (ISBN 1-934259-04-7)

Grappa, Ove Boudin (ISBN 91-633-1351-0)

Greek Salad, Mile Lambert-Gocs (ISBN 1-189267-82-5)

Harry Waugh's Wine Diary, Harry Waugh (ISBN 0-932664-53-9)

How and Why to Build a Wine Cellar, Richard Gold (ISBN 978-1-891267-00-0)

Hungary, David Copp (ISBN 963-86759-6-9)

I Supertuscan, Carlo Gambi (ISBN 88-88482-40-7)

Icon: Art of the Wine Label, Jeffrey Caldewey and Chuck House (ISBN 1-891267-30-2)

Imagery: Art for Wine, Bob Nugent (ISBN 1-891267-30-2)

In Celebration of Wine and Life, Richard R. Lamb and Ernest Mittelberger, (ISBN 0-932664-13-X)

Journey Among the Great Wines of Sicily, Carlo Gambi (ISBN 88-88482-10-5)

Making Sense of Wine Tasting, Alan Young (ISBN 978-1-891267-03-1)

Napa Wine: A History, Charles L. Sullivan (ISBN 1-891267-07-8)

New Adventures in Wine Cookery (ISBN 1-891267-71-X)

The New Italy, Daniele Cernelli and Marco Sabellico (ISBN 1-891267-32-9)

New Wines of Spain, Tony Lord (ISBN 0-932664-59-8)

Northern Wine Works, 2nd ed. Thomas A. Plocher (ISBN 1-934259-18-7)

Olive Oil, Leonardo Romanelli (ISBN 1-891267-55-8)

Oregon Eco-Friendly Wine, Clive Michelsen (ISBN 91-975326-4-9)

Pasta, Fabrizio Ungaro (ISBN 1-891267-56-6)

Piedmont, Carlo Gambi (ISBN 88-88482-43-1)

Pleasures of the Canary Islands, Ann and Larry Walker (ISBN 0-932664-75-X)

Po Folks Favorite Recipes, William I. Kaufman (ISBN 0-932664-50-4)

Pocket Encyclopedia of American Wine, Northwest, William I. Kaufman (ISBN 0-932664-58-X)

Pocket Encyclopedia of California Wine, William I. Kaufman (ISBN 0-932664-42-3)

Portugal's Wines & Wine Makers, New Revised Edition, Richard Mason (ISBN 1-891267-01-9)

Prosciutto, Carla Bardi (ISBN 1-891267-54-X)

Red & White, Max Allen (ISBN 1-891267-37-X)

Rhone Renaissance, Remington Norman (ISBN 0-932664-95-4)

Rich, Rare & Red, Ben Howkins (ISBN 1-891267-63-9)

Rum, Dave Broom (ISBN 1-891267-62-0)

Sauternes, Jeffrey Benson and Alastair McKenzie (ISBN 0-856673-60-9)

The Science of Healthy Drinking, Gene Ford (ISBN 1-891267-47-7)

Secrets of Chilean Cuisine, Robert Marin (956-316-014-2)

Secrets of Patagonian Barbecue, Robert Marin (956-316-015-0)

Secrets of Peruvian Cuisine, Emilio Peschiera (956-8077-71-5)

The Taste of Wine, Emile Peynaud (ISBN 0-932664-64-4)

Tasting & Grading Wine, Clive Michelsen (ISBN 9-197532-60-6)

Terroir, James E. Wilson (ISBN 1-891267-22-1)

Tokaj, David Copp (ISBN 963-87524-3-2)

Understanding Wine Technology, David Bird (ISBN 1-891267-91-4)

The University Wine Course, Marian Baldy (ISBN 0-932664-69-5)

Vine Lines, Wine Cartoons, Judy Valon (ISBN 978-1-891267-93-2)

White Burgundy, Christopher Fielden (ISBN 0-932664-62-8)

The Wine Buyer's Record Book, Ralph Steadman (ISBN 0-932664-98-9)

A Wine Growers' Guide, Philip M. Wagner (ISBN 0-932664-92-X)

Wine Heritage, Dick Rosano (ISBN 1-891267-13-2)

Wine in Everyday Cooking, Patricia Ballard ((ISBN 0-932664-45-8)

Wine, Food & the Good Life, Arlene Mueller and Dorothy Indelicato (ISBN 0-932664-85-0)

Wine Investment for Portfolio Diversification, Mahesh Kumar (ISBN 1-891267-84-1)

Wine Lovers Cookbook, Malcolm R. Herbert (ISBN 0-932664-82-2)

Wine Marketing & Sales, Paul Wagner, Janeen Olsen, Liz Thach (ISBN 978-1-891267-99-X)

Winery Technology & Operations, Yair Margalit (ISBN 0-932664-66-0)

The Wines of Baja California, Ralph Amey (ISBN 1-891267-65-5)

The Wines of France, Clive Coates (ISBN 1-891267-14-0)

Woody's Liquid Kitchen, Hayden Wood (ISBN 0975212397)

World Encyclopedia of Champagne & Sparkling Wine, Tom Stevenson (ISBN 1-891267-61-2)

Zinfandel, Cathleen Francisco (ISBN 1-891267-15-9)

Making Sense of Wine Tasting: Your Essential Guide to Enjoying Wine, Fifth Edition

Text copyright © 2010 Alan Young

First published in 1986 by Greenhouse Publications Pty, Ltd.

The Wine Appreciation Guild
360 Swift Avenue
South San Francisco, CA 94080
(650) 866-3020
www.wineappreciation.com

Designed by Tony Cooper & Alan Young
Fifth Editon Updated by Diane Spencer Hume
Cartoons by Paul Rigby
Illustrations by Gary Chen

Library of Congress Cataloging-in-Publication Data

Young, Alan.
  Making sense of wine tasting : your essential guide to enjoying wine / Alan Young ; foreword by
Miguel Torres.
     p. cm.
Includes bibliographical references and index.
ISBN-13: 978-1-891267-03-1
ISBN-10: 1-891267-03-5
1. Wine tasting. I. Title.
TP548.5.A5Y684 2007
641.2'2--dc22

CONTENTS

DEDICATION

To the memory of Diana Cullen. A rural Australian lady who stood tallest among her peers. First of all as a Mother, then as a winemaker of rare talent who brought world fame to the Margaret River, Western Australia wine region.

From the typing of the first draft to the final editing of the finished manuscript, many women have made generous contributions to this book. I can think of nothing more fitting than to also dedicate this work to women wine lovers of the world. This fifth international edition honours six other wonderful women who have given so much to literature and wine:

Norma S.Young, Elaine F. Barry, Helen Martin-Beck, Wendy Cooper, Ann C. Noble and Deidre Tronson.

FOREWORD

Alan Young has a different view of wine than most other writers. He discounts the usual romance and insists on facts that honestly expose wine truthfully to the end consumer. I have seen this while working with him on his book about our wonderful wine industry in Catalonia, as well as reading this fifth edition of the classic, *Making Sense of Wine*.

Alan started his wine career as an involuntary vine pruner 61 years ago in 1943, made his first wine in 1951 and has been a consumer longer than most readers have been alive. His wine education programs have taken him to most wine producing countries—from Israel to Uruguay. Alan, with his wife Norma, has been a guest in my Chilean home and at my winery in Catalonia many times.

This fifth edition of *Making Sense of Wine* is a truly remarkable study of our present wine education knowledge and is more like a wine library than one single book. As the author illustrates, we don't really taste wine, rather we look at it, smell it, put it in our mouth and all these thousands of signals rush to the brain and in a micro-second we have a remarkable multi-sensorial picture of our likes and dislikes of all features of that wine.

Moreover, this work is the first wine book that explains, in considerable depth, how our brain works in making decisions for each individual who puts a glass of wine to their eyes, nose or mouth. Chapters on how the nervous system and the brain convey these signals are for professional or beginning wine aficionados who really want to maximise their wine knowledge. Yet, that is not necessary for everyone.

The author has made this edition a **speed read** for those who want only the basic facts of wine understanding. Throughout the book these paragraphs are highlighted and are summarized at the end of each Chapter. All the technical writing, graphs and charts can be bypassed and the reader will still obtain maximum pleasure and knowledge from this work.

I truly believe that every wine lover, regardless of where they live, will obtain all the knowledge of sensory evaluation they require from this book

—Miguel Torres

ACKNOWLEDGMENTS

The author and publisher wish to acknowledge the following organisations and publishers for permission to use their materials:

Nick Lena of Gretag Macbeth, 617 Little Britain Road, New Windsor, NY 12553.

American Wine Society Journal for the quote on page 157.

Professor Ann C. Noble for the Aroma Wheel on page 66.

The International Food Information Council Foundation for portions of the taste chapter on page 106.

The Ishihara company, in absentia, for the work on page 13.

PREFACE

This book sets out to teach you that wine, like anything else that gives us pleasure, can be enjoyed more fully by those who have taken the trouble to learn something about it, and who have tried to develop their individual sensory systems. The human sensory system, which includes sight, smell, touch, taste and hearing, can be trained, just as our minds or muscles can be trained. In fact, a high level of assessment skill is within reach of the average wine lover. There is no mystique about this, regardless of what the snobs and poseurs say.

What is sensory evaluation? Very simply, it means using the senses of sight, smell, touch and taste to make an evaluation of food or beverages. For example, we use our sense of hearing to evaluate sound.

The need for a totally new type of wine book first occurred to me in 1981 when I was invited by Les Amis du Vin to present 24 Australian wine seminars in 20 US states.

This was an unforgettable experience. It was easy to accept that the hundreds of wine lovers who attended these seminars knew nothing about Australian wines, surprisingly however, they had a considerable knowledge of European wines and vineyards. But it was their complete lack of knowledge about the components of wine and the criteria for discriminating between good and ordinary wine which was of interest to me. During the seminar discussions it became obvious that these wine lovers had a great desire to acquire this knowledge.

In subsequent seminars in the USA and other countries in Europe and Asia, I found that this desire for basic knowledge was not only widespread but also international. This prompted the foundation of the International Wine Academy, by a group of dedicated professionals including myself, which now presents seminars in Australia, Argentina, Canada, China, Germany, Hong Kong, Israel, Italy, New Zealand, South Africa, Thailand and the USA.

In the quest for answers to questions regarding the basics of wine judgements, I found that highly respected wine authorities were presenting evaluations and descriptions in such terms as 'we tasted horizontally the two best vintages of the 1970s; one wine tended to be the lightest, most open and forward. Another had more backbone, closer consistency, greater length, while a third was broad, meaty, a bigger earthier wine.' Here's another example: 'I would say the wine soared upwards in an assertive curve to a high point, on this level its finesse and subtlety registering a deeply frilled set of waves, before the gradual droop, always with an accompanying slight up-peaking at each decline of the flavour'. While some wine people may understand this jargon, others may think that they are descriptions for a garage-door, rather than great wines.

What information do such statements convey? Many of these statements are sheer gobbledygook and intimidation, even to those with long involvement in the wine industry. What do they, or could they, mean to the uninitiated? The wine literature abounds with metaphors and cliches but it is very difficult to find hard facts about the nature of the wines discussed.

I have found it necessary to go right outside the wine industry to find people with answers to questions in the specialist fields of colour, sight, lighting, smell, taste, physiology and psychology. This search has roamed from one end of the globe to the other—to universities, eye clinics, lighting suppliers, perfume houses, apiaries and a wide variety of research centres.

This study has unearthed much new information from these sources and should greatly enrich our knowledge and understanding of wine and food evaluation. Some of the answers have provided a firm basis for what I already believed; some have been quite startling in their revelations and must force us to rethink many of our assumptions. Unfortunately many more important questions about food and beverage evaluation remain unanswered, and may remain so for many more years. Fundamental to the enquiry is the issue of what and how our senses perceive and it is for this reason I commend to you the more technical aspects of this work, particularly the understanding of the workings of the human brain, our own personal computer that still has no peer in today's sophisticated hi-tech world.

Appreciation of so many things we cherish—music, art, films, literature, men, women—is conditioned by the observations that we have fed into our brain, and it is with our 'conditioned' brain that we interpret what we see, hear, taste and feel. We do not make decisions or judgements in isolation—it is our environmentally and culturally conditioned brain that makes these decisions and judgements. By understanding the conditioning and workings of this incredible piece of our body we can enjoy our wine and, indeed, our whole life, far more.

This book presents a serious, and often very technical, discussion of the nature and role of colour, smell, touch and taste in the evaluation of wine. These all form part of our total response to wine and interrelate to each other in a far more complex and sophisticated fashion than has previously been believed. As will be explained, a bright color, for example, is not a pleasant bonus in wine that is otherwise good or bad, it is necessarily part of its quality. We know that steak that is greenish is bad, we know that a wine that is cloudy is defective. We need to examine the role of color, and likewise the roles of smell, touch and taste in the process of wine evaluation.

Furthermore, we need to investigate the nature of taste. Do smell, touch and colour affect our evaluation of taste? It is such issues as these that this book sets out systematically to explore. It is in this context that I have produced a wine book that addresses itself to such unfamiliar areas as neurons, cilia, nanometers, kelvin, geosmin, diacetyl, olfaction, gustation and the like.

The chapters not only examine the operation of the various sense perceptions but also provide the reader with an array of exercises and procedures for developing and testing the evaluation skills discussed throughout the book.

Literally hundreds of people have contributed to this work. They will all know the parts they have played and the gratitude felt regarding their help. It must be put on record, however, that the whole project would have been quite impossible without the help and resources of International Flavors and Fragrances and its officers in many parts of the world.

Individually, enormous support came from Professors Lindsay Aitken and Elaine Barry of Monash University, Melbourne; Ann C. Noble; University of California, Davis; and the late Morley R. Kare and his staff at the Monell Chemical Senses Center, Philadelphia, Paul Rigby then in New York.

In this edition my warmest thanks go to Dr. Deidre Tronson at UWS, Dr. T. Jacobs, Cardiff University, and Nick Lena of Gretag Macbeth. As ever, Peter Saunders, Tony and Wendy Cooper were magnificent in their unfailing support.

It is hard to believe that Helen Martin-Beck had the courage to type and retype hundreds of pages for this book, but, ever smiling, she despatched pages across continents from her Perth , Western Australia base. Many friends around the world were generous enough to continually provide transport and home cooking as I combed the world for answers to questions that are the concern of all devoted wine and food lovers. Editor, vigneron and wine lover, Sue Mackinnon, finally shaped thousands of words into a readable first manuscript—now in its fifth edition.

The fifth edition is a masterpiece of the publisher's art. In addition to this first full-colour printing, the cooperation and expertise shown by all at Wine Appreciation Guild has been stunning. Cheers to Elliott, Donna and Bryan

To all those, wherever they may be, who helped—thank you.

—Alan Young,
San Francisco, California

A sobering thought:

We are at the beginning of an era where we can interact with the brain. We can apply what we know about brain plasticity to train it to alter behaviour. People are always trying to find ways to improve learning.

—Professor Hubert Dinse
German Scientist

INTRODUCTION

Winemaking is very much like painting.

The appreciation of painting is either subjective, 'I don't know much about art but I know what I like' or objective, based on some genuine knowledge of what the artist is trying to convey. It is this latter kind that leads us to deeper and more subtle levels of understanding. As in any other field of human endeavour, knowledge opens up new horizons.

Winemakers, like painters, start with a range of basic materials: soil, grapes, climate. Yet these essential elements can change dramatically in less than a mile, let alone across nations or oceans. A Cabernet grape, for example, grown in Canada, near the New York State border, or on the island of Tasmania, will provide very different flavours from the same variety grown in the warmer climes of Algeria or Texas.

Add to this the variables of the winemaker's art whether to pick grapes earlier or later, use SO_2 or not, leave the 'must' on skins longer or shorter, whether to ferment the wine in barrels. The possibilities are endless. Then there is the range of equipment; irrigation systems, mechanical harvesters, fermentation tanks of wood, stainless steel and concrete, centrifuges, diatomaceous earth filters, tank presses, vertical drainers. Here too the possibilities are endless.

It's only necessary for the wine lover to tour Australia's Barossa Valley or Hermansburg, Missouri, USA, Spain's Catalonia, France's Midi—or Alba, Italy, noting the amazing variations of equipment being used by winemakers to achieve a common end, to understand why wines are so different. We've come a long way from the old bacchanalian treading of the harvest.

For a full appreciation of wine we need to know something about all these things just as the art lover extends his response to art by understanding the varying elements that create it. Above all we need to know something about how our senses guide us in the appreciation of wine or food. Most of what we know about the world around us we learn from our senses.

Despite enormous advances in scientific knowledge, technology and chemical analysis over the past half century, wine can still only be properly assessed by human sensory evaluations, i.e. sight, smell, touch and taste—*as variable as this is from one person to another*. In any exhibition wine is judged by humans, not by machines; well not yet.

This, of course, leaves the door open to the charlatan, whether he be the winemaker charging exorbitant prices for poor quality in the hope that the lofty price tag will impress, or the wine snob who summarily condemns new wine styles, or wine from certain areas, producers or processes. One should always be wary of the 'knocker' who goes in for generalized judgements, 'Irrigated areas can't produce good table wines', or, 'Only French wines are worth tasting' and the 'expert' who can't justify his judgement in specific language: 'It's a naive domestic Burgundy without any breeding, but I think you'll be amused by its presumption.' (Thank you, James Thurber!)

The human element in sensory evaluation also leaves the door open to simple relativism—the idea that, because our senses are subjective, one person's opinion is as good as the next and there can be no objective judgement at all. It's the 'I don't know much about art but I know what I like' theory applied to wine. Certainly no wine critic or winemaker can talk about quality in relation to your own taste; if you taste a wine as bitter, then it is bitter—regardless of what others say or think.

And certainly wine can be enjoyed by anyone, even those who know nothing of its components. A quality wine can be defined generally as one free of measurable faults and one that gives us pleasure; a wine either gives us pleasure, or it does not—regardless of what others may say or think.

But we should be aware at the outset that our concept of quality has much to do with our habits and upbringing, with products with which we are familiar or comfortable. With wine, habit tends to lead us to well-known brands and familiar tastes.

Of course, there is a positive place for the well promoted label. In most cases, these are carefully researched 'popular' tastes that will not offend, that are reliable, inexpensive and likely to win people over to wine. In fact, such *vins de table* styles are the wines most of us drink with our everyday meals. Not even the most ardent wine lovers want to drink champagne and eat caviar every time they sit down to dinner. Nor could they afford to. And this brings up another determining factor on quality—price.

Much potential appreciation of wine is killed by sheer monetary consideration; most wine lovers just cannot afford or justify expensive wines. To produce high quality distinctive wines requires expensive grapes—Cabernet, Chardonnay, Pinot, Riesling, etc.—and for the red wines (and some whites) lots of new oak casks costing a small fortune. Such wines must command premium prices; however these expensive wines are not necessary to develop skill and judgement in wine evaluation and appreciation.

The traditional 'goodies' from Australia, California, France and New Zealand have gone through the ceiling for most of us not on expense accounts. This means that we turn our attention to the undiscovered delights of Argentina, Australia, Chile, Germany, Italy, Canada, South Africa, Spain, the unfashionable and lesser 'growths'. Be adventurous in your wine purchases. Try those 'strange' labels from Catalonia, Curico, Washington State or Western Australia. That way you will obtain maximum pleasure from this work and, maybe, you will discover some unknown great wines; I do regularly.

And it's here that the challenge of learning how to appraise wines, understand new flavours, varieties and treatments, is worthwhile; the search for quality at an affordable price. While the axiom 'you get what you pay for' may still be largely true (though I'm afraid price no longer necessarily equates with quality), and while it is common for the uninitiated to make positive responses to expensive wines, they could generally obtain equal pleasure from an unknown $5–10 wine.

Some price snobs may decide the quality of the wine when they see the $6 sticker. Chances are that their assessment would be different if they tasted the wine before seeing the price. Then a 'bad' wine may be assessed as 'good value' or a 'bargain' with the wine being tasted on its merits, rather than the price dictating the assessment.

For the proper training of our sensory perceptions in regard to wine, three things are necessary.

First, knowledge about how our various senses respond, and how wine appeals to them. ***That knowledge is the basic concern of this book.*** Second, the development of a disciplined concentration which can identify minute traces of chemical substances and a host of other wine components, and a memory that will recall taste and odour characteristics. ***Just as our muscles can be trained, so can our senses.***

These two are interrelated; inability to concentrate will quickly kill the memory. It is for this reason that most professional wine judgements are made early in the day when our senses are sharpest and we are less liable to interruptions. Fatigue, noise, flashing lights, highly perfumed flowers (or people) and other distractions are not conducive to objective evaluation.

Thirdly, the use of *precise* language. It is often difficult to relate to terms in which wine is described—cuddly, elegant, delicate, cheeky, pretentious, foul, etc.—which are so personal and so vague that they are virtually meaningless. Yet no one can tell what is good or bad about a wine until he or she can put a name to it. When names describe objective qualities of wine it then becomes possible for one person to communicate his or her experiences to another, and the learning process is hastened and enjoyed.

Precise language

During your study of this text you will notice that the words taste, flavour, touch, palate and sweetness, in particular, come under close scrutiny. Over the years, these absolutely fundamental words of sensory appraisal have been brought into common usage somewhat removed from their real meanings as we know them today.

Now is a good time to set the record straight. While some people will have difficulty adjusting, I'm proposing that these words be carefully examined and then used in their correct context for sensory evaluation.

For the student who wants to speed-read or just get to the very essential points of a chapter, these points have been highlighted in yellow throughout the text—and again in a summary at the end of each chapter.

Important message

CHAPTER 1

—From the brilliant pen of Paul Rigby

QUALITY

Quality is an intellectual phenomenon that occurs between the wine and the taster; it is independently related to neither.

—Richard Nelson Ph.D., Canada

DEFINING QUALITY

At seminars around the world, many wine lovers are astonished when asked to define quality. But, until we each determine our own concept of quality it is extremely difficult, if not impossible, to make an evaluation—sensory or otherwise—of anything. As ridiculous as this sounds, few people can verbalise their opinion of quality. Can you?

What is a quality restaurant (as opposed to a pretentious restaurant), a quality automobile, suit of clothes, wine or meal? Or quality anything? And who sets the standards for quality? Let's look at an obvious source—*Webster's Dictionary*—for the answer:

1 *A characteristic or attribute of something: property; a feature.*

2 *The natural or essential character of something.*

3 *Excellence; superiority.*

4 *Degree or grade of excellence.*

5 *(a) A high social position. (b) People of high social positions.*

Frankly, none of these come anywhere near my concept of quality, and, if you check a selection of those submitted by wine lovers who have attended my courses around the world you'll possibly agree that Dr. Richard Nelson's definition is incredibly accurate: 'Quality is an intellectual phenomenon that occurs between the wine and the taster.'

Intellectual phenomenon

Here's what some of my students have to say about the subject:

1 A standard of acceptance at my current level of development.

2 An objective standard of excellence, with an absence of technical faults.

3 A measurement of the extent to which an item satisfies one of the senses.

Most people would agree that quality is a double-sided coin — quality should have both physical and psychological attributes.

Without Fault

Nearly all physical commodities—wine, clothing, automobiles, furniture etc., are made to a set of standard specifications enabling us to measure whether the product is free of measurable faults. A surprising number of students consider that a quality article *may* have a measurable fault. Part of the appeal of handmade furniture or pottery, one might say, is the irregularity that proclaims the hand of its maker. Yet this is not a virtue we would seek in other products—a car, food or clothes. For my money, a wine (or any other product) wearing an expensive price tag must be faultless to earn quality recognition.

Anticipation and Expectation

The psychological aspect of quality rests in anticipation and expectation. We preset standards for almost any activity in which we participate; if the event or product lives up to our expectations it's fairly sure that we will give it top quality rating.

Dr. Ann C. Noble, has this to say: *Since quality is a composite response to the sensory properties of the wine, based on our expectations which have been developed from our previous experiences with a wide range of wines and our own personal preferences, this judgement is an individual response. No two people integrate the individual attributes in the same way, much less have the same preferences.*

I think that statement is worth re-reading—and remembering.

All wine evaluation is about a search for quality. It is an attempt to negotiate the disputed territory between objective standards and personal preferences.

We don't judge our favorite jug red in the same category as we judge a top Australian Syrah any more than we would judge a Jeep in terms of a Rolls Royce, although both may be recognised as quality products. They're aimed at different social occasions, different people and different prices! Our expectations have begun to define our concept of quality by setting up relevant categories of judgement. Cost may well be a factor here. Within such general categories, further expectations are set up by our own experience. Allowances may be made for brilliant intuition, but on the whole the greater our range of experience—in wine, as in art or music or literature—the better our judgement, and the more authoritative our sense of quality is likely to be.

Anticipation plays a part in enjoyment and appreciation of all human activity from sex to fishing or listening to music. Anticipation can be misleading—as witnessed by the hordes of *label-drinkers*—but, if properly developed, it can be a positive factor in determining quality. Indeed it is one of the arguments of this book that the anticipation of a wine—what its sight and smell say to us before we ever put it in our mouth—is a large measure of our joy in it.

Measurable faults

Definition of Quality

Anticipation

Visual Stimuli

During my sensory evaluation seminars, a variety of slides are shown to test reactions to some artistic, humorous and landscape visual stimuli. The students are asked to tick an adjective. These are the responses, which show the culture, received from similar sized groups in various cities: Atlanta, Georgia and Jackson Hole, Wyoming, USA; Adelaide; Australia.

	Boring	Pleasing	Humorous	Nothing	Intriguing	Exciting	Offensive
Slide 1							
Atlanta GA	1	15	1	1	1	0	1
Adelaide Aus	2	0	5	4	5	1	0
Jackson Wy	3	0	15	0	3	0	0
Slide 2							
Atlanta GA	0	3	12	0	4	0	1
Adelaide Aus	0	1	15	0	2	0	0
Jackson Wy	2	0	12	5	1	0	0
Slide 3							
Atlanta GA	2	4	0	4	7	3	0
Adelaide Aus	0	1	2	4	9	1	0
Jackson Wy	1	1	3	2	9	4	0
Slide 4							
Atlanta GA	1	1	1	2	8	2	5
Adelaide Aus	0	1	8	0	7	2	2
Jackson Wy	1	0	2	3	8	0	1
Slide 5							
Atlanta GA	3	1	1	5	2	0	8
Adelaide Aus	0	1	8	0	7	2	2
Jackson Wy	3	2	2	5	7	0	0

Look at how we think

Just look at those Atlanta people? Slides 1 and 2 were cartoons from famous Australian, Paul Rigby. Slides 3, 4 and 5 were Dali paintings that certainly drew positive responses across the choice of adjectives. I don't really know that Dali would have been overjoyed at the 'Boring' and 'Nothing' responses or even the number of people who thought his work was offensive.

Dali paintings

This is but a small example of how our brain is conditioned to one set of visual stimuli.

Whatever you do, don't be browbeaten or intimidated by fancy labels or prices; write down your own definition of quality. One thing is certain, it will definitely change with your socio-economic ups and downs!

VARIABILITY OF PERCEPTION

Very simply, sensory evaluation means using the senses of sight and smell, touch and taste to make evaluations of food or beverages.

The problem with so many judgments is that our emotions and cultural prejudices are used rather than our senses.

Here is a hypothetical case. A two car head-on collision happens right in front of six people standing at a bus stop. One driver is badly injured. The six people were: the wife of the badly injured driver; an insurance agent; an attorney; a tow truck operator, a body shop owner and a reporter.

Did these people all see the same accident?

Defining Sensory Evaluation

Physically their eyes saw the same thing. By the time the visual images were processed through their brain, each person saw a totally different situation. Here the individual emotions and financial rewards or losses, rather than the senses, came into action.

Noted California winemaker, the late Louis M Martini is on record as saying, *We like best that with which we are familiar.*

This introduces the judgmental problems of religious and cultural preferences. Regardless of whether a product is good or bad, each religion and culture has its own doctrine classifying that product.

Political and socio-economic affiliations may also determine one's acceptance or rejection of a product.

The Hypothesis

The brain is the source of all our dreams, our moods, our thoughts, our actions. The brain is three pounds (1.36kg) or more of tens of billions of nerve cells (neurons) and many more billions of glial (supporting) cells. Its ceaseless day and night activity needs massive amounts of oxygen and calories, derived mainly from glucose. These, as well as other necessities such as amino acids, ions and hormones, are transported or diffused across the protective blood-brain-barrier into the brain.

The complexity of the inter-connections of these billions of nerve cells and their ability to process information defies the imagination. It is estimated that some of them may have ten thousand or more connections with other neurons.

Chemical Senses

Brain input from smell and taste (*the chemical senses*) receptors are now known to affect not only olfaction (smell) and gustation (taste) but also behaviour, memory and learning, various emotional states and possibly other activities essential to both mental and physical well-being.

It seems reasonable to suggest, therefore, that in the coming decades further advances of the neurosciences will clarify not only the way the brain handles information coming from the chemical senses but also their role, along with that of nutrition, in the normal functioning of the brain and in the prevention and treatment of disturbed mental function.

Human actions are ultimately the net result of decisions made by the central nervous system resulting from many input channels. The effect of inputs is presumed to differ from *individual to individual.* In other words, whether we *cut* our finger, *see* a great painting, *hear* a superb orchestra or *taste* an excellent glass of wine—all sensations travel to the cerebral cortex for interpretation, judgment and decisions; the *reactions* occur in the finger, the eye, the ear or the mouth, but only after orders (the motor signals) from the brain have returned to the point of contact.

When we cut a finger, a message flashes to the brain, the sense of pain speeds to the finger and another complex mechanism files away a message telling you to be more careful next time you use a sharp knife. Some people make a major performance of a cut finger, others ignore the same problem. If you think that your personal computer is really something then consider the capacity of your brain, it can store zillions of pieces of worthwhile information and trivia for instant recall.

Sense of Pain

Smell—Olfaction

Our knowledge of the mechanism of smell is far from complete. Some of the most important odour information processing takes place within the mucous layer of the olfactory epithelium at the top of the nasal cavity. Odour molecules link to specialized receptor sites (lock and key molecules—see Olfactory chapter pages 51–83 on the membranes of the hairline cilia attached to the millions of smell neurons found there. It is not yet known whether there are specific receptors for specific odours, but we do know that olfactory receptors can monitor the environment with great precision. Humans, as well as many other animals, can distinguish odour due to quite small variations in the chemical structures of the odour molecule.

Our knowledge of the mechanism of taste is greater than that of smell, but it is still incomplete. The common perception of flavour is actually a combination of *odour* and *taste* inputs plus *texture* and *temperature.* Here we are concerned only with the five basic tastes bitter, salt, sour, sugar and umami.

Great Precision

Taste—Gustation

Taste and smell *interact* closely in determining our appreciation of food and wine. Early man utilized the sense of taste to monitor poisons, that were often bitter, from calorically valuable foods which tended to be sweet. Taste is important for modern man as well. Many diseases, medications and other therapies interfere with our ability to taste. Most of those so affected lose any interest in eating. Frequently they develop psychiatric disturbances in addition to physical deterioration.

Taste perception begins with specific receptor cells in the taste buds located primarily on the tongue but all around the *oral cavity.* While numerous, the taste receptors are far less in number than the smell (olfactory) receptors. Unlike the olfactory receptors, the taste receptors are not themselves neurons but connect with neurons whose processes lead to the brain.

Psychiatric Disturbances

All of this fascinated the writer and sent him off to all parts of the world to try and understand these many things that he, and his wine loving friends, did not understand. It was all new and technical and needed to be understood by the average wine or food aficionado.

A threshold study (Young 1988) of six Champagne makers was made in Epernay, France, considered by the French to be the home of sparkling wine. The study, consisting of probably the five top winemakers in the region, looked at the individual perceptions of these people evaluating the basic wine components: acid, sugar, alcohol, acid+sugar, acid+sugar+alcohol.

On a scale of 10 their perceptions, from one individual to another, varied from 0 to 10 and these people were recognised as being the best! This helps to explaining why one winemaker (or any individual) will say that a wine has too much acid while another individual will indicate that the same wine has too little acid. See results of Champagne tests on pages 8–9.

This partially clarifies the difference between individuals, while another study (Young, 1987) indicates the differences between cultural groups. A total of 27 wines from eight countries was judged by experienced panels of 14 judges. The judging of identically the same wines from the same case took place in Beaune, France; London UK, New York and San Francisco USA and Nuriootpa, Australia.

The wines, all Chardonnay, came from: Australia 5; Bulgaria 1; California 4; Chile 1, France 11, Italy 2, New York 1, New Zealand 1 and Spain 1.

In each country, judges were asked to nominate the best 12 wines. The panel of Burgundy winemakers selected six Burgundy wines in their top 12 and rated the two lowest-priced wines as #1 and #2. The London panel chose but one Burgundy wine, the most expensive, in their top 12.

None of the three US or Australian panels chose one Burgundy wine in their selections. Only two California and two Australian wines were chosen by all five panels as being worthy of the top 12.

Another two studies by Young et al 1986 and 1987, showed the difference between consumers and professionals.

The wines of each Australian state and New Zealand were judged by four categories of panels:

1. Female consumers	2. Female professionals;
3. Male consumers;	4. Male professionals;

The 1986 panels each comprised three members while the 1987 panels had four members each. Completely separate panels judged all the wines submitted from their *own state only*, or New Zealand.

The best three wines in each of seven red and 11 white categories were then sent to an international judging in Melbourne (1986) and Adelaide (1987). For the international judging, the same four categories of judging panels were comprised of people from five Australian states and New Zealand.

At the conclusion of the judgings in which more than 2000 wines and 150 judges participated, all score sheets were sent to the Chisholm Institute of Technology (now Monash University) for statistical analysis.

The main areas of study were:

a. Individual wines: mean score; mean score by sub-groups; range of marks; maximum and minimum marks.

b. General: Kendall Coefficient of concordance; list by mean rank— total and sub-groups ; list by mean score—total and sub-groups; mean score for all wines: red and white table wines separately.

After thorough analysis, the most important conclusions were:

- *Consumers and professionals have entirely different criteria as to what represents quality.*
- *There is less than five percent chance that consumers and professionals will select the same wine as being the best in any class.*
- *There is decidedly more consensus among consumers than among professionals. This poses the question," Is one professional judgment worthwhile?" If so, which one?*

Professionals versus consumers

In some areas, this might be considered as old data but subsequent similar events conducted in Adelaide, South Australia, major events in the 21st century have substantiated these figures—with the exception that the professionals have raised their game to agree with consumers about seven percent of the time!

Don't be intimidated

It is of the utmost importance that either the wine or other judges should not, at anytime, intimidate the wine lover. Wine is a very personal thing.

Understanding that we are not born equal, or the same, this in no way detracts from the fact that there are certain objective criteria in wine (or food) evaluation. And, certainly, the more we learn—the more we are able to appreciate the sensory delights of wine.

These objective criteria are:
- **Sight**—appearance and colour.
- **Smell**—aroma and bouquet.
- **Touch**—feel, texture, body/viscosity.
- **Taste**—sugar, salt, acid, bitter.
- **Flavour**—a combination of smell, touch, taste.
- **Structure**—mouth °feel , a combination of the touch and taste senses.
- **Balance**—a fusion of all the above in-mouth sensations.
- **Evolution**—ageing, maturation, bottle development.

Before making any judgment of a given wine, remember that the wine represents at least one year, and possibly up to five years, of the winemakers life. Do not dismiss a wine without considering what the winemaker was trying to express. Some considerations might be:

Considerations

- A $6 Chilean wine made from three-year-old vines compared with a $100 French wine made from 25-year-old vines.
- Some winemakers do not like oaked wines, but you do. The winemaker is trying to show the fruit of the wine for early consumption; who's right?
- Wine made in a year of bad climatic conditions such as excessive rain or drought against a wine made in a year of good climate.

These, and other factors, will affect the perceived quality of the wine.

All the above matters are dealt with at length in succeeding chapters.

It can be seen from the foregoing that there is a wide range of perceptions and understandings about all facets of wine. It could be said that there is no *right* way or *wrong* way; rather there is *my* way and *your* way.

Results of tests with Champagne makers

WINE 4		ANALYSIS BY 7 JUDGES SIX CHAMPAGNE MAKERS AND THE AUTHOR						
	JUDGES	EM	MM	MG	FLB	AL	JC	AY
VISUAL	Pale				■			
	Moderate				■			
	Gold	■			■			
	Dull							
	Brilliant	■			■			
MOUSSE	Big							
	Small	■						
	Persistant		■			■		
	Creamy							
FRUIT	Missing		■	■				
	Identifiable							■
	Moderate							
	Good	■			■	■		
	Intense							
AROMA	Floral					■		
	Citrus				■			■
	Biscuit	■						
	Apple/Pear							
	Other		■					
YEAST	Missing					■		
	Light				■			
	Moderate							
	Balanced							
	Excessive							
ACID	Lacking							
	Moderate					■		
	Balanced	■	■	■				
	Excessive							
TECHNIQUE	Dirty							
	Clean	■		■			■	
	Simple							■
	Well made		■			■		
	Complex							
LENGTH	Short		■					
	Medium				■		■	
	Long	■						
AFTER TASTE	Nothing							
	Clean							
	Short		■		■			
	Medium	■				■	■	
	Lingering							

TASTE SENSE	ANALYSIS OF 5 CHAMPAGNE MAKERS		EM	MM	MG	FLB	JC
ACID	TEETH	Upper	4	4	3	7	4
		Lower	4	4	3	3	3
	GUMS	Upper	3	7	4	9	5
		Lower	3	6	3	5	9
	LIPS	Upper		3	2	3	8
		Lower		3	2	5	8
	TONGUE	Tip	6	6	4	4	8
		Top	6	6	4	6	8
		Sides	6	8	8	5	
	CHEEKS	Front	4	7	8	4	3
		Rear	5	6	6	7	2
	THROAT		3	5	3	7	3
SUGAR	TEETH	Upper	1	4	2	7	3
		Lower	1	4	2	7	3
	GUMS	Upper	1	4	2	8	7
		Lower	1	4	3	7	7
	LIPS	Upper	1	5	2	6	7
		Lower	1	5	2	8	7
	TONGUE	Tip	8	6	8	4	7
		Top	8	8	6	3	
		Sides	7	7	4	9	
	CHEEKS	Front	2	7	3	6	5
		Rear	2	6	6	8	5
	THROAT		1	8	5	7	6
SUGAR / ACID	TEETH	Upper	2	4	2	8	7
		Lower	2	4	2	3	3
	GUMS	Upper	2	5	4	7	7
		Lower	2	5	3	4	
	LIPS	Upper	3	4	2	6	8
		Lower	3	4	2	7	7
	TONGUE	Tip	8	6	5	4	8
		Top	8	7	3	6	6
		Sides	8	8	6	4	
	CHEEKS	Front	7	7	8	8	6
		Rear	7	7	7	8	6
	THROAT		1	8	3	8	4
TACTILE	TEETH	Uper	2	4	2	7	2
		Lower	2	4	2	8	2
	GUMS	Upper	4	6	3	6	4
		Lower	4	5	3	8	4
	LIPS	Upper	3	5	3	5	2
		Lower	3	5	3	7	2
	TONGUE	Tip	4	5	4	7	1
		Top	6	7	6	9	
		Sides	6	7	5	6	
	CHEEKS	Front	3	7	7	6	2
		Rear	3	8	6	8	2
	THROAT		3	8	5	10	2

Results of
tests with
Champagne
makers

COLOUR SCALE
Pink   = 0
Blue   = 1-3
Green   = 4-6
Red   = 7-10

CHAPTER 2

We do not see with our eyes alone; we need light so that our eyes may form images of objects—and a brain to interpret the meanings of the nerve impulses.

Figure 1. A winter jogger and light confusion

What this 7am San Francisco winter-jogger thinks he sees is the set of traffic signals on the left, but what he really sees is the set on the right. If the green light was really green, many people would not be able to distinguish its colour, so a healthy dose of blue has been added to traffic lights around the world to avoid confusion between red and green.

SIGHT

The marketing side of the international wine industry thrives and drives on lies, lies and more damned lies. How many examples does one need? Go to your local wine store and read a few back labels, you'll be amazed at what the human mind can imagine?

In fact, industry critics and observers have, for so long, been nothing less than cavalier in their comments about sight and colour, and it is very obvious that this important factor has not been generally studied. Many major companies such as Nestles, Frito-Lay, General Mills, General Foods etc., have all identified, through consumer testing, that colour and appearance of product are as important to a consumer's perception of product quality as taste and smell.

What food critic would make an assessment of food without considering the appeal of sight and colour on the plate? Wine and food go hand-in-hand.

"Let's just rush ahead and smell and taste the wine—why worry about colour and appearance (or touch)" Those strange folks using the 100 point system don't care about colour or sight anyhow. More about this later.

Bright colours and appearance are not an added bonus in wine, they are an essential part of the quality.

This is highlighted by the absurdity that almost 100% of teachers and commentators recommend that wines be judged against a bright white or white background, which is a totally wrong scientific proposition. Are we just followers of someone else's written word and too lazy to do some basic research; or even worse, check the facts?

The American National Standards Institute (ANSI) specifies that colour evaluation must be made in booths or surrounds of the grey colour N8—while the American Society of Testing Materials (ASTM) states N7 is their choice. Other colour industry people use backgrounds varying from N5–N8. N1 is black and N9 white, see Figure 2.

Light and colour authorities

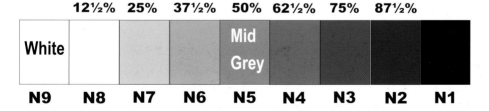

Figure 2. Defining grey/gray and colour *value*.

Wine colour is so vitally important that should a wine lose even half a point (on the 20 point scale) during this judgement, the wine has almost no chance of winning a gold medal in any competition. But then again, very few judges are trained in the importance of colour and sight so they use a 100-point scale as a throw-away system.

Amazing
human eye

Colour: Excellent work done during the 1970s at the Australian Wine Research Institute and repeated in 2002 at the Centre for Advanced Food Sciences at the University of Western Sydney, Australia, has proven that red wine quality can be correctly judged by colour alone using sophisticated spectrophotometers.

Due to a built-in constant light source, these machines are capable of greater accuracy with greater reliability than the amazing human eye—which is capable of more than seven million colour discriminations.

Sight through the human eyes comes from two types of visual receptors—rods and cones. About one hundred and twenty million rods allow us to see at night. Somewhere between five and seven million cones in the retina of the eye allow us to have colour vision.

This colour vision we are born with stays with us, with very little change, during our lifetime. However, a good pair of untrained eyes is of modest use. Many factors such as individual colour deficiency, appropriate lighting, useful glassware all come into the picture. What do you see in Figure 3?

However, sight and colour training can be of enormous use to any wine lover, training that will definitely benefit your own daily lifestyle as well.

Colour
deficiency

There are various levels of colour deficiency that are linked to the X chromosome. Since males have a single X chromosome (inherited from their mothers) and females have two (one inherited from each parent), colour deficient vision occurs in one of 12 males—but only one of 250 females.

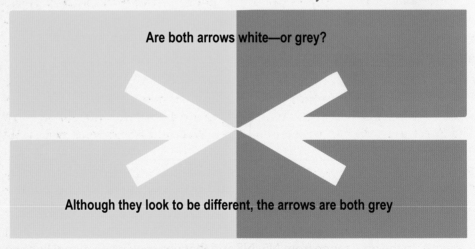

Are both arrows white—or grey?

Although they look to be different, the arrows are both grey

Figure 3. Simultaneous contrast

Deutans
Protans
Tritans

Colour deficient vision is caused by a partial or complete absence of one or more of the three types of cones. The most common form of colour deficient vision is partial green defectiveness. These individuals are called Deutans if they have a total absence of green receptors. The second most common colour deficiency is partial red vision. Protans have all red receptors missing while Tritans are missing blue receptors. A Monochromat has only one type of cone. Just imagine the problems that Protans have in judging a rare from well-done steak or other meats?

Deutans and Protans really have problems with red and green, which has more than a nuisance value for those individuals during wine and food assessment.

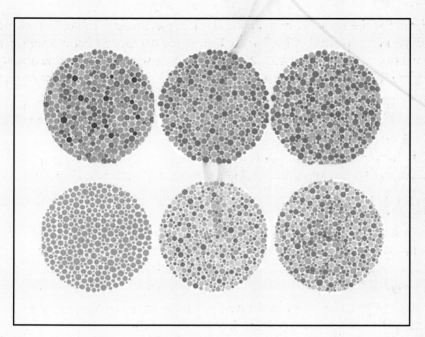

Figure 4. Ishihara colour "blind" test. What numbers do you see here? From top left the numbers are: 56, 45, 29, 25, 6 and 8.

While surround sound may be one of today's hot items, surrounding colour or simultaneous contrast plays an important role in wine evaluation.

ASTM D1729 states that a range of N5 to N7 is acceptable. In ISO 3664 for the Graphic Arts, a range of N5 to N8 is acceptable. The real issue is not the lightness or darkness of the surround but that it is *truly* a neutral grey.

Gretag Macbeth, the world's leaders in this field, use N7 in their SpectraLight Products and N8 in the Judge® and Prooflite® booths. The lighter colors were chosen only because darker grey made the booths appear smaller. The SpectraLight® has been in use since 1976 and works very well in all applications.

Regarding the choice of daylight, filtered tungsten is far better than any fluorescent source for evaluating color—filtered tungsten halogen is the best by far.

So, if you are considering establishing a wine evaluation booth, it is best that you paint in the grey range from N5–N8 and that you seek professional lighting help from Gretag Macbeth at one of their offices in the USA, Switzerland, UK, Germany, Hong Kong or Italy. Obtain further details from their website: www.gretagmacbeth.com. This is not a paid advertisement—just the result of a long and helpful association. Gretag Macbeth have provided most of the technical material for this chapter plus several of the illustrations.

Bear in mind that darker grey can make the wine booths appear smaller.

Perception Training

Perception is the complete process of receiving information through one of the senses, comparing this information with past experiences, identifying it,

Concentration

Colour training

The Eskimos

and evaluating it. Visual perception is a skill we learn while growing up; it does not appear immediately in a newborn infant.

It will be repeatedly said in this text that the brain is selective in the information that it filters for storage and recall. As in the other aspects of appraisal (smell, touch, pain, taste) only those subjects that we concentrate on, and train ourselves in, will be stored away for future recall. Training in colour discrimination during everyday activities will improve our ability to discern colours, and their meaning in wine. Just look out the window and see how many shades of green you can isolate. How many whites, reds and browns surround you? And what effect does light and shade have on colours as you see them on your way to and from work or from your office or kitchen window?

Make the training more scientifically controlled by experimenting at home with a few bottles of food colouring. Half fill four glasses with water, add a few drops of red colouring to one glass, double the number in the next glass. There will only be a slight difference in saturation, keep adding drops until you obtain a deep red. Now add one drop, then another, of blue and note the changing tints. In the other glasses add yellow colouring in the same proportions, then add a drop of green. Intensify the colours and then ask a friend to bring you random glasses to test your powers of discrimination. Apart from a general enlargement of our aesthetic responses, the underlying premise of such training is a recognition of the importance of colour in wine evaluation.

Our language reflects our limitations. The Eskimos are reputed to have over 40 words for snow; reflecting the extraordinary ability to discriminate within the dominant colour of their culture, whereas dwellers in more temperate regions are severely limited in their perception and language. Think of how many words you know for yellow? Why do we call a white wine *white*, when that is one colour that it is not! Colourless, green, yellow, gold, straw maybe, but not white.

Colour Can Damn

On one occasion I attended a vintage port tasting, in Boston, with a group of experienced tasters, many professional, and I was flabbergasted that, after 13 wines, not one of the group mentioned the colour of any wine in their comments, even though the best wine in each 'flight' was obvious from its colour alone. The 'in mouth' evaluation of these wines did nothing but confirm what was apparent from the visual appearance.

An indication of the importance of colour and appearance in wine is the importance placed on these two factors in wine competitions. They are always an explicit component of the score, generally about 15–20 per cent, (I think it should be 40 per cent), thus an extra half point scored in this section of the judging can make the difference between earning a gold or silver award. But, on the other hand, a competition wine can be rejected by the judges on colour or clarity alone, without any further appraisal. Colour can be this damning!

Most competition wines are scored on a 'modified' U.C. Davis system. There are several of these, one which we determined in the 1970s and have constantly modified to keep it abreast of changing times:

Sight—colour and appearance	maximum four points
Aroma and bouquet	maximum six points
In mouth	maximum six points.
After flavour	maximum two points
Overall	maximum two points
	Making a total of 20 points

The normal allocation of points for awards is: Bronze 15.5–16.9, Silver 17.0–18.4, Gold 18.5–20. Forget all about the 100 point system!

Even for the layman, colour and appearance are crucial parts of the total aesthetic appreciation of wine. It is my fervent desire to stand on the roof of every city hall in the world and shout aloud, *'wine is all about colour and smell''*.

Colour's crucial role

To the sceptic, intent on drinking as much as possible, who declares that it is all about taste, I would point out that, technically, the oral cavity (don't only talk about the tongue) can register only five taste sensations: sugar, sour, salt, bitter and umami (as explained in following chapters). What we normally call 'taste' is very largely smell and touch which, when combined with taste, makes up the overall flavour impression.

Music is a good analogy of discrimination. The difference between a good and a brilliant performance is the ability of the musician to interpret the nuances of the composer's finer points. Equally, the skill of the wine judge can be measured by his or her ability to interpret the nuances of colour and appearance. Colour and appearance are the first important aspects of wine appraisal—the starting point for *harmony* in wine, when colour, smell and flavour are perfectly integrated.

Wine judges skills

ORIGINS OF COLOUR IN WINE

Colour in wine comes mainly from two sources—grape skins and oxidation. The pH and sulfur dioxide levels in the must and wine dominate the net contribution from these sources.

The juice colour of most winemaking grapes is similar to lemon juice. Very few varieties have pink or red juice. The colour and character of all red wines comes from the skins. The red pigments of wine grapes are called anthocyanins and these, with related phenolic compounds, are derived by extraction during fermentation.

Juice colour

These compounds are what differentiate, in the senses of sight, smell, touch and taste, red wine from white wine. The style and character of a particular wine are largely determined by the quantity and condition of the phenolic compounds, including anthocyanins. As much as 5g/liter of total phenolics may be present in a young, red wine, but the anthocyanin level will rarely reach 1g/liter.

All anthocyanins are derivatives of the basic flavylium cation structure and it is the flavylium cation that gives anthocyanins their colour. At a pH of 3.4 to 3.6, 20 to 25 per cent of the anthocyanins in wine are the coloured flavylium cation form, while only 10 per cent exist in the cationic form at a pH of 4.0. This provides us with the ability to measure quality by colour alone.

The second source of colour is oxidation, which is the enzyme-mediated action of oxygen substrates, primarily phenols, in the fruit or juice. Oxidation is the brown discolouration that appears when we cut an apple or pear (and so many other fruits and vegetables). Grape juice and wine suffer the same browning when exposed to uncontrolled oxygen.

Other than in small amounts, oxidation is, generally, a fault in wine. Sherries and some table wines are aged in oak barrels under conditions of controlled oxidation; this is, in most cases, a desirable situation. Although grape skins and oxidation are the two primary sources of wine colour, there can be other factors affecting colour that the evaluator should know about. Briefly, these are:

The grape variety. Some grape varieties have higher concentrations of pigment in their skin. We expect a Cabernet Sauvignon, Zinfandel or Syrah to be a deeper colour, 'thicker', than Pinot noir or Gamay grapes.

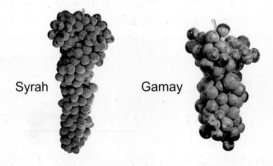

Syrah   Gamay

The maturity of fruit. Colour builds up as the fruit approaches optimum ripeness. Beyond that point colour starts to deteriorate as the skins break down.

Climatic zones. The chemical balance of cool climate fruit is different from the same variety grown in a warm region. Grape skin thickness can vary from six to fifteen per cent of total grape weight. Thicker skins are consistent with cooler climates thus providing more phenolics (pigments and tannins) during fermentation.

Soils. Soils rich in iron produce a more scarlet colour, as do warm, dry summers.

Fermentation techniques. It is during the primary fermentation, when the grape sugars are converted into alcohol (ethanol) and CO_2 that the wine style will first be determined. The length of time the winemaker leaves the red/ black skins in contact with the fermenting juice really dictates the style and colour. Higher temperature fermentations, around 25–28°C (80–90°F), will be responsible for quicker extraction of phenolics.

Daily 'pumping over" and/or "punching-down'. Pumping the juice over the skins is a major contributor to colour extraction, otherwise the skins, called the cap, sit on top of the juice and no extraction takes place. Punching-down the cap has the same beneficial effect.

The reaction of anthocyanins and tannins. While anthocyanins are the most important pigments in young red wines, they are progressively incorporated into polymeric tannin-type materials with ageing, and the tannin itself becomes a pigment with a brick red colour that typifies an ageing red wine.

Sulfur dioxide. Research work by Dr. T.C. Somers at the Australian Wine Research Institute during the 1970s suggests that wine colour (and consequently wine quality) is dominated by pH and sulfur dioxide (SO_2) levels. While the technicalities of these factors is beyond the scope of this book, they may be summarized by saying that it is desirable for table wines to contain a low pH, and therefore high acid levels, while at the same time having acceptably low levels of SO_2. High pH is responsible for less vibrant colour as the chemical form of the pigment moves to violet or colourless form. As pH increases, so hydrogen ions dissociate to produce anions- these are more prone to oxidation thereby increasing the need for SO_2, the primary anti-microbial agent in winemaking .

Importance of SO_2

Oak barrels: Prior to going into barrels, grapes such as Chardonnay, Chenin, Sauvignon and Semillon become yellow-gold colours when fully ripe. This can be enhanced by some hours of contact (maceration) with the ripe skins. However, this practice is now mainly out of vogue as it also drops the pH of the juice significantly.

Oak barrels

Sight extraction from the barrel staves during maturation/evolution, plus limited amounts of oxygen during the process, all contribute to a deeper saturation of colour.

Ageing/evolution. Like people, all wines should change with age. (These are not necessarily positive changes!) Red wines get progressively less intense, passing from red through ruby, brick red, to mahogany, then tawny and finally amber brown.

At this stage the colour of the wine is solely the colour of the tannins, the anthocyanins are long gone. White wines, on the other hand, through oxidation grow darker with age moving from straw to golden shades, then brown, and finally to a maple syrup colour.

The range of red and white wine colours

THEORY OF JUDGING COLOUR AND APPEARANCE

Any colour can be described by making use of three attributes, hue, chroma and value. In the textile, dyestuffs or paint industries, for example, these attributes are:

Hue

This is the red, yellow, green and blue (or intermediate between adjacent pairs of these) tints that comprise our wine colour. Black, white and neutral grey have no hue. In a 'blind' tasting—or one held under red lights—only a small percentage (20–30 per cent) of tasters can tell the difference between red and white wine; this is simply a lack of training in the sense of *touch*. So, when we can see wine in good light, we should pay particular attention to the various aspects of sight since they are not only part of the aesthetic enjoyment of wine, but a valuable guide to its quality.

Red and white wine

Chroma and Value

Chroma is very close to what some people call saturation. Chroma is the strength or weakness of a colour. In commercial paint applications, we take a can of white base and add red pigment – and this gives us a pink.

As we continue to add pigment we are increasing the percentage of red and increasing the chroma, which increases from pink to red. The hue naturally stays the same.

Value is the lightness or darkness of a colour based on a perfect white having a value of 10 and a perfect black having a value of 0. The Value will change with the addition of red colourant. The higher concentration or percentage of red pigment will yield the same *hue* but a darker colour or lower value.

Hue stays the same because we have the same starting point and are only adding a single red colourant.

Value changes as a function of the pigment percentage and the darkness of the mixture.

Red wines, for example, can vary from a light rosé to a deep purple depending on wine style, the term 'red' being almost as loose as 'white'. Density of colour can be related to 'body' in a wine, full-bodied being thicker, darker than 'light bodied' wines. The winemaker's use of sulfur dioxide is relevant here. While a certain amount of SO_2 may be a good thing to prevent oxidation and bacterial spoilage, excessive use of it will bleach wine colour.

Density of colour

It is not uncommon to observe a wine six to ten years old that has absolutely no natural colour development. White wines that do not show saturation of colour from four to five years of age will, more likely, give off offensive odours (mainly SO_2) during the olfactory appraisal.

Brightness is another factor in *sight*. Technically, brightness applies to an object that emits or reflects light. Brightness is an important part of clarity (see below), yet as an aspect of sight, especially in wine, it goes further. Relevant terms are brilliant, sparkling (non bubbly), as distinct from cloudy, dull, opaque. One might think of it as the difference between glass (clear) and diamonds (sparkling). All good wines—even an aged red—should be bright. Brightness is a visual sign of well-being in wine; a dull or flat appearance suggests decrepitude or high pH.

Clarity

The other important aspect of appearance is clarity. Modern-day technology has provided the means to make all wines clear and bright, to the stage that almost anything, including colour, can be filtered out of the wine. This is both good and bad.

At several stages during processing, from the crushing of the grapes to pressing the fermented skins, the must (fermented juice) looks like thick soup—minestrone, French onion or pea soup, depending on your individual preference. By a series of cleaning-up processes—fining with eggs, colloidal clay or dried bull's blood, filtration through diatomaceous earth or sterile pad or just through natural settlement and racking—the finished wine is bottled free of any visual impurities.

Even in the clearest juice there lay lurking bacterial microbes waiting for a particular set of circumstances to spoil the wine. The spoilage agents may have been in the new bottles, corks, filtering equipment or the filtered wine. While there can be numerous harmless, visible particles in wine, the average consumer does not like the sight of them when opening a bottle during a social occasion.

The best example is an unstabilised white wine that could produce harmless tartrate crystals after refrigeration. Their similarity to Epsom salts—or chips of glass—is off-putting! Yet many of today's most expensive wines are sold unfiltered and this is considered by many wine lovers to be a sign of high quality.

The first visual examination is the very surface of the wine. Here can be found several tell-tale signs of bad wine health. Check to see if the surface is oily, milky or clear.

Turbidity

In simple terms, turbidity is the opposite of clarity. It is particulate matter, the material that causes haze or turbidity and protects microbes from the killing action of disinfectants that gives us bacterial spoilage. For this reason the winemaker eliminates every possibility of turbidity. The American public health authority defines turbidity as 'an expression of the optical property that

Minestrone soup

Optical properties

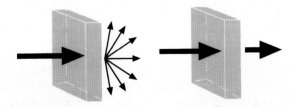

Figure 4. Light passing through turbid and clear samples

causes light to be scattered and absorbed rather than transmitted in straight lines through the sample'. This scattering and absorption is caused by the interaction of light with particles suspended into the samples. Clay, microbes, organic matter, and other fine, insoluble particles can cause turbidity. Turbid samples have a hazy or cloudy appearance.

Although there are hundreds of millions of bottles of wine processed each year, faults are rare. Most wine lovers never see a bad bottle of wine. But just to alert you to the possibility, here's how to go about checking your wine for clarity. An unpleasant 'nose' will accompany many of the visual defects. First, look at the surface of the wine as it can reveal much information. Well-made wines, from small or large wineries, are normally sparkling bright or even brilliant in appearance.

Cloudy or dull wines

Any sign of haze, smokiness, milkiness or oily surface should be regarded with suspicion. Cloudy or dull wines are usually spoiled with bacterial infection, yeast proteins, pectins or maybe metal salts. With today's technology, most wines, particularly white table wines, are stabilized before bottling. This is a process designed to eliminate, by chilling and filtering, harmless tartrates and to create the clarity and brilliance we expect from good wines.

Wine diamonds

The demand for clarity is not incompatible with the desirable sediment we find in good reds and some ports. Just as red wines take their colour and tannins from the grape skins, both the colour pigments and tannins can precipitate in the bottle and become sediment in table wines and vintage ports. Tawny and ruby ports in the barrel prior to bottling deposit this sediment, which starts to precipitate after about three years.

Suspended material

The tartrate crystals that are normally removed by stabilisation in white wines form on the inside of the barrels and become known as wine 'stones' or 'diamonds'. Frankly, I find it encouraging seeing the phenolic sediment adhering to the side of a red wine bottle, this being an indication that the wine has not been over-processed and that some of the real natural grape elements are still intact.

Visually Apparent Faults

Having said that, for the purpose of pointing out that all sediment and suspended material is not indicative of poor quality, most other visual impairments are to be regarded with the utmost caution. It is not the scope of this work to examine in detail the numerous origins of these faults—but some of the main ones are listed below.

Bacterial spoilage is the principal cause of cloudy-looking wines, and you can accept my word that such wines will not be good for anything—and that includes marinating meat or salads!

Active lactic acid bacteria in sweet wines will leave a silky sheen or haze when the glass is swirled and the wine may develop an oily opalescence. It is almost impossible to remove all yeast cells after fermentation (although we are coming closer to that technology) and if there is sugar in the final product, the cells can spring to life again and begin secondary fermentation.

A source of smokiness in whites and dullness in reds can be malolactic fermentation taking place in the bottle, one of winemaking's love-hate syndromes. In cool climate high-acid wines, it is desirable to convert the coarse malic acid of the grape to the softer lactic acid, thereby reducing total acidity. But, in warm growing regions where a goodly portion of total acidity is respired from the fruit before picking, this secondary fermentation that further reduces acidity, is not really welcome. It takes away 'life' from the wine, leaving it 'flat' and without appeal. Should this take place in the bottle rather than beforehand, several problems can arise.

The first, a build up of carbon dioxide in the bottle will create a similar effect to 'sparkling burgundy' when poured; secondly, the wine will be cloudy. Wines with this, not unusual, fault may eventually settle to a clear state over a period of three or more years without any deterioration of quality.

Secondary fermentation

Healthy Visual Signs

Bubbles are generally a healthy sign; they are the great delight of sparkling wines—'beaded bubbles winking at the brim' as Keats noted. The bubbles in wine are carbon dioxide gas, created in sparkling wine at considerable expense. In still white wines bubbles are what the Germans call 'spritzig' and the French 'pétillant' and are a sure sign that the wine has been carefully handled (but no guarantee of quality) at bottling time. To avoid the traumas of oxidation, new bottles are purged of oxygen by inert gas prior to filling. Wine in the storage tanks is held under a blanket of gas, once again, to keep it free of the enemy oxygen. As white wines are bottled very cold, some of this gas is taken into solution and appears in the bottom of the glass when poured.

Bubbles

Not all bubbles are born equal. On the credit side, we make our first visual decision of sparkling wine by the size of the bubbles. Small and continuous bubbles are normally associated with high quality. Poorly made sparklers normally have big, fat irregular bubbles.

Away from the favoured Italian Lambrusco, bubbles in red wine should be regarded akin to a time bomb. These bubbles can be accompanied by a cloudy/milky appearance, which suggests that the wine has undergone malo-lactic fermentation (MLF) in the bottle. Almost without exception, wines that are dull, hazy or milky will be almost undrinkable.

Legs or tears are another phenomenon associated with the visual aspects of wine. There is probably more nonsense written and spoken about 'legs or tears' than any other facet of appraisal; maybe because it's the first of the fallacies that the novice learns about. The most common myth is that these tears running down the sides of the glass indicate high alcohol wines. False! It's only necessary to take a nip of brandy (40 per cent by volume alcohol), swirl it in your glass and you'll notice that the legs are almost non-existent.

Legs & tears

Yet take an ounce or two of a sweet white table wine at 10 per cent by volume of alcohol, swirl that in your glass and you have real legs. The answer comes in two parts—first is the difference in surface tension between water and alcohol, the second is the viscosity of the wines, the differential evaporation of alcohol, sugar and glycerols combining with the wine. All in all, legs and tears are best kept out of wine talk; most wine people find it a subject of little interest.

OBSERVING COLOUR—LIGHTING

To achieve maximum results in evaluating wine colour we need the best available lighting. Few people have it—most will never use it because, as yet, there is no such thing as standard lighting for wine assessment. Lighting specialists know much about illumination; wine people know little or nothing of the light needed for evaluation. We talk about daylight as though it was a standard commodity—nothing could be further from the truth! Daylight is different in the morning, noon and afternoon; clear blue skies vary dramatically in light value to overcast skies; lighting in the Northern Hemisphere is much softer than the world below the equator. Lighting studies indicate that colourists, artists, and the like, prefer the light from a natural, moderately overcast north sky.

Daylight is different

The production of colour requires three things: a source of light, an object that it illuminates, and the eye and the brain to perceive it. This is where we run into the first problem—subjectivity—colour exists only in the mind of the viewer. The relative insensitivity of the eye limits the visible part of the spectrum to a very narrow band of wavelengths, between 380 and 750 nanometers: a nanometer being a unit of wavelength. One nm = 1/1,000,000 mm, and there are 25 mm to one inch.

At the bottom end of the scale we start with violet (380–440 nm), blue (440–490), green (480–560), yellow (560–590), orange (590–630) and red (630–700). Hues are not really clear-cut as they blend into each other, as blue-greens, green-yellows all along the spectrum. Purple is a mixture of red and blue from opposite ends of the spectrum. At wavelengths below 390 nanometers we have ultraviolet light and X-rays, while above the red hue there is infra-red and radio waves.

Metamerism or Flair

If the light source changes, the stimulus to the brain differs and we can expect the perceived colour to differ also. So we have a situation where a suit buyer selects a brown suit in a store with warm tungsten lights only to find that in daylight the suit will be another colour! This phenomenon is known as metamerism or flair, and has an important role in wine colour assessment. Indeed, it is the cardinal reason that wine judging should have a standard light source. By definition metamerism is 'a change in observed colour depending on the nature of the illuminating light'.

Tungsten & daylight

If we take three colours of different pigments, A, B and C, that, for the normal sighted, will match under one light source, we find that, say, under daylight conditions, colours A and B will match and C will be the odd colour. But when we view the same colours under cool white fluorescent, B and C will match and A will be the odd one. Yet, if the same three colours are viewed under incandescent lighting, none of the three will match! This is illustrated on page 40.

The amazing phenomenon of metamerism, combined with the known facts that the perception of colour varies from one person to another, and that we don't have an accepted standard light source for wine appraisal, leads us to all sorts of conjecture. While the one constant attribute of wine colour is the wine itself, the other two elements of colour perception—the source of illumination and the perceiver—are changing with each appraisal.

Nowhere has this been more evident than in the round of Australian wine competitions which produce lottery-like results annually. (Other international competitions produce similar variations). Australia has, by far, the most frequent and competitive wine contests and for the 'down-under' winemaker success in these contests is money in the bank. Two similar competitions for young red wines are held back to back in the cities of Brisbane and Melbourne. Wines from the same vintage batch are entered simultaneously in each contest. The Melbourne contest attracts between 300–600 entries for the young red wine event alone, and the overall Melbourne competition draws more than 3000 entries.

Australian wine competitons

Although two different companies have won one of the competitions for three consecutive years, no one has ever won both competitions with the same wine, submitted to the same specifications and judged within 2 weeks!

Variation in Light Source

How can we explain this anomaly? Certainly the human element is one variable; different judging panels operate in each city. But most of the judges are extremely competent winemakers (although I don't know that any of them has been colour tested!). However, the real variable—one that is never mentioned—is the lighting; there is no standard light source for wine contests. In addition, there is climatic variation, which we will deal with in the chapter on smell. Over 1000 miles further north, Brisbane is considerably warmer than Melbourne, providing superior conditions for olfactory evaluation.

Just as wine components have many strange forms of measurement (percentage by volume or percentage proof alcohol), degrees *brix* or *baume* for sugar, grams per litre for sugar, cyanide etc., lighting's measurement is temperature in degrees Kelvin. The vast difference in the various light sources is reflected below:

Different lighting standards

Kerosene Lantern Wick	2000°K
Incandescent Light	2850°K
Cool White Fluorescent	5000°K
Daylight Macbeth	7500°K

The three important factors here are:

- What wavelengths of the spectrum does each include?
- How do the light sources compare with each other?
- In what areas of the colour spectrum are they the same?

This is where disaster strikes anyone making colour judgments of wine.

**International
standards**

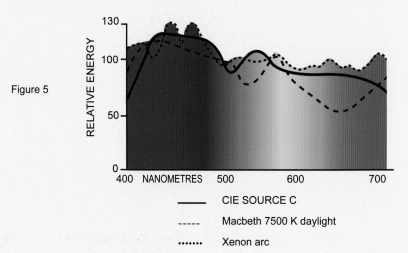

Figure 5

CIE SOURCE C

----- Macbeth 7500 K daylight

······· Xenon arc

**Natural
daylight**

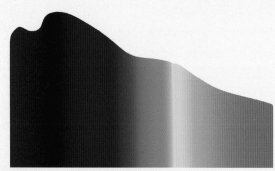

Figure 6

Curve A—Natural Daylight
Natural preferred North Sky Daylight at
7400 Kelvin. Note that it contains a
good balance or energy throughout the
entire range of the visible spectrum.

**Filtered
light**

Figure 7

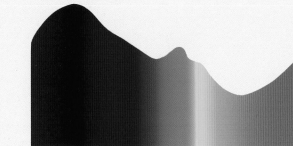

**Curve B—Macbeth Filtered
Daylight 'Spectralight'®**
Note how closely this curve reproduces
that of natural North Sky Daylight
across the entire visible spectrum.

Average
daylight

Figure 8

Curve C—Average Daylight Fluorescent
Note the abrupt changes of the
fluorescent simulations versus the smooth
flow of the natural daylight curve.

Blended daylight

Figure 9

Curve D—Macbeth Blended Daylight 'Examolite'®
This is the blend of special fluorescent
tubes and incandescent bulbs. It is also
a balanced energy source and is, again,
a good simulation of natural daylight.

Ordinary
incandescent
light

Figure 10

Curve E—Ordinary Incandescent Light
Here you will note the very high
predominance in the red-yellow range of
the spectrum as compared to the green-blue-
violet range.

As there is no constant standard natural daylight, the world authority on illumination, the French-based Commission International de l'Eclairage (CIE), has determined a standard that is shown as the continuous heavy black line in figure 5; Xenon arc, which is shown as the small dotted line, follows the CIE recommendation rather closely, but what is sold as daylight fluorescent, shown by the broken line, falls apart in our areas of vital concern, more particularly in the red wine zone, and to a lesser extent in the green-yellow area.

Gretag Macbeth has been working on this problem for more than 100 years to provide a standard, and the best possible duplication of natural daylight for artists, colourists and others who work in the field of critical colour matching. Over this long period, they've learnt that no fluorescent lamp has yet been made that can provide this lighting. Macbeth says that the only commercially feasible way to simulate light of daylight quality is with filtered tungsten lamps ref. ASTM Standard D 0 1729–69 (74).

And, if you want a bad light source for wine evaluation, the candle is about as bad as you can get! (It may be OK for wine clarity but not for colour.)

Problems

I think these graphic examples explain the need for a standard light source, but I'm not the authority to do that. All I can do is warn of the obvious deficiency of human perception, something that is common to all nationalities. About this, we can do nothing. But, the subject of standardised lighting, which will help minimise this problem, is within our resources; let's have some action—18 years later—nothing!! This is a contributing factor in many of our crazy wine competition results—and nobody cares.

WHAT IS DAYLIGHT?

What is daylight?

Natural daylight is variable. Lighting studies indicate that colourists, artists, finishers, etc. prefer the light from a natural moderately overcast *north* sky. Colour analysis of this light is shown in Figure 6. Note all colours are present in the light and that there is a little more blue than in the others, which accounts for the bluish characteristics of the North Sky Daylight. Figure 6 represents the ideal with which light sources are compared to determine how well the artificial source can be substituted for the natural one.

Since 1915, Macbeth has offered artificial daylight sources for critical colour work. The colour analysis for Gretag Macbeth Daylight as provided in the Macbeth Spectralight unit is shown in figure 7. Critical colour matching is the name applied to initial formulation of colour compounds to match a given sample, requires lighting which is the best possible duplication of natural daylight. The only commercially feasible way to closely simulate light of this quality is with filtered tungsten lamps. (Ref. ASTM Standard D-1729–69(74). No fluorescent lamp has ever been devised which can do the job as well, because even the special, colour-balanced fluorescent lamps emit high energy peaks of certain colours. These peaks mislead your colour judgment because that judgment is rooted in the 'smooth curve' characteristics of natural light. You can see these peaks very plainly in the accompanying figures 8, 9 and 10.

Note the smooth flow of the natural daylight figure 6 versus the abrupt changes of the fluorescent simulation (figure 8). It's a bit like the effect you get when tuning your AM radio—the more distant stations vary slightly in their signal strengths but when you hit the frequencies of local stations, your ears are blasted by the sudden high energy peaks. So it is with your eyes: they're blasted by the sudden peaks of energy which are present in all fluorescent lighting.

The argument that critical colour matching should be done under fluorescent lamps simply because the finished object will someday be viewed under fluorescent lamps, has no basis in fact. There is no more validity to this reasoning than there is to the thought that raincoats should be manufactured in the rain because they will someday be worn in the rain.

For less exacting work such as shading, grading, inspection, etc, GretagMacbeth offers the low cost Examolite® Fixture. This type of illumination is a blend of specially engineered Examolite colour corrected fluorescent tubes and Examolite 'long life' incandescent bulbs. The curve of the Examolite blend is shown in figure 9 and represents the highest degree of colour corrected 'simulated' daylight available with a fluorescent source.

Figures 8 and 10 represent ordinary fluorescent and incandescent light. Both of these lights have colour rendering deficiencies.

THE VISUAL EXAMINATION

Having carefully chosen the best available glassware (see pages 47–49) and the best available lighting, we now need an area devoid of strong colours that could reflect or conflict with the wine colours. It is desirable and possible to have N7 and/or N8 grey as a background but in most instances it is sufficient to have a white tablecloth. If possible, try for a grey tablecloth.

There are four positions from which wine colour can be examined:

1. I try to make evaluations as the wine is poured from the bottle—while it is between bottle and glass—looking at the wine as it's poured, or as it splashes in the glass. This is not easy and it requires a lot of concentration. Why not try this every time you see wine poured; a good background of light grey/buff helps.

2. The most common everyday appraisal is when the glass of wine sits on the table and is viewed obliquely against a favourable background.

3. For critical analysis, rotate the glass quickly, swirling the wine so that it climbs up the side of the glass and look through the swirling wine; this will reveal any giveaway brown signs of premature ageing. (At the same time the swirling wine coats the total surface of the glass readying it for the olfactory appraisal.)

4. Tilt the glass away from you so that a tongue of wine reaches the very rim of the glass. For red wine appraisal, I use a champagne flute. A flute allows for a long tongue—and this is what must be examined. Here the heart and soul of wine colour is exposed.

Special lighting

Figure 11

FLAIR. The same observer can find that the same object is a different colour when viewed under a different light source. This is called *'flair.'*

Examples of flair and metamerism

Figure 12

METAMERISM. An observer will often find that pairs of colours with different spectral curves will match under one light but not under another.

Purity

First, look for the purity of colour—has a young red or white wine any of the spoilt factors that were discussed on pages 19–20. Check to see that there is no 'watery' rim around the edges, or on the tip of the tongue. Quality red wines with cellaring potential will have pure colour right to the meniscus—the very tip of the tongue and along the sides. Young white wines should be free of any brownish signs of oxidation.

Saturation/chroma

Colour chroma is our next concern as this will indicate the body or viscosity of the wine. If in doubt, go back and check page 18.

Appearance

Now, let us look at the appearance of the wine, starting with the surface, followed by the brightness of the wine. Record your observations on a score sheet, preferably the one recommended on page 33 (figure 13) which will ensure that you don't skip any of the fundamentals. Proceed with a preliminary olfactory and then a quick 'in mouth' appraisal, *solely* for the purpose of confirming your visual observations.

Having smelled, felt and tasted the wine, go back to the visual aspects and check the relationship of colour-viscosity, colour-acidity, colour-nose, colour-flavour and colour-length of after-flavour. Look at the wine, think about each of these factors and next time you are speaking to a winemaker (or similar experienced person) discuss your findings. This is all a learned response requiring much application, lots of practice and concentration. Make sure that you spit out your taste samples, otherwise all wine will eventually look and taste great!

A word of warning! There are many so-called 'experts' who will tell you that colour has no association with wine quality. I can only say that if you follow the above procedures, you will arrive at a very different conclusion; one that the world's leading researchers have determined.

Visual observations

RED TABLE WINES

Young red table wines should have brilliant tints of red/scarlet/purple, depending on the growing region, grape variety, fruit maturity and condition.

As red wines age, both table and fortified styles progressively pass through the colours of ruby, mahogany and tawny as the colour pigments precipitate. Amber-brown is an acceptable colour; brown is one to be treated with the utmost caution.

While colour must always remain subjective, anything that approaches 'dirty' brown—such as the oxidised apple or pear—is very much a minus factor. Orange browns that could be considered visually pleasing are usually indicative of good condition. However, aged coffee or chocolate coloured wines are an acquired taste and one should not necessarily like a brown wine just because it is aged. Wines of superior quality will always carry colour to the very edge of the tongue, and it is my studied belief that this is the first sign of a top class product.

During the ageing of red wines, there is some precipitation of tannins, tartrates and pigments—this is no problem, in fact, this becomes the sediment in wines. Most people prefer to decant wine from this sediment before serving. (There is a minority who prefer to keep the sediment, and, after disposing of the wine, enjoy the sediment with freshly dug truffles!)

Orange browns

Among the normal ageing deposits we are likely to find tartaric acid crystals (wine diamonds) resting on the bottom of the bottle or, sometimes swimming around in solution. These are quite normal in vintage ports, red and some white wines.

The term red covers almost every colour from scarlet purple to the palest tawny—and each tint tells its own story. Reading these colours requires practice and experience—much experience—but as the average wine lover confines his or her imbibing pleasures to a limited number of styles and regions, this knowledge, by application and concentration, can be quickly gained. (You get out what you put in!) It's a different story for the professional judge whose skills must cover all districts and styles.

WHITE TABLE WINES

White table wines range across the yellow colours from pale straw/yellow (like lemon juice) to rich gold, depending mainly on fruit ripeness and age of the wine. In a young wine, deeper colours will indicate ripe fruit and, possibly, some skin contact which will be further enhanced to deep gold tones with age.

Experience

Cool area wines will often have a green tint. Perhaps this is chlorophyll—maybe unripe fruit. If the wine is overly acid, lacking in flavour (as opposed to sugar) you can bet this is due to unripe fruit.

Above all, young white wines must be clear and brilliant; like diamonds. There are no ifs or buts about this statement. The ageing process will lessen this to a glasslike brightness.

Evaluating white wines for colour and appearance is the extreme test. While *colour* is important, the critical test is the appearance and this can rarely be done by looking at your own wines; look at the ones on either side of you.

Cool areas

Very few people in an evaluation/judging or tasting session are sitting in similar light, look around the room at other people's glasses—even stand up and see how different each person's glasses appear to your own.

Most function rooms have a window and there may be other light sources in the room other than the main light source (see photo on page 56 which has daylight coming from the left side, at the rear are two incandescent lights and diffused daylight enters from the front of the photo). These will all reflect in the glasses and give many points of view. Judging white wines for colour and appearance is a very difficult task that requires lots of practice.

Traditionally, many Italian and Spanish winemakers have kept their white wines in oak barrels for several years prior to bottling, thus acquiring the unaccustomed, strong and unpleasant oxidative characters. Although, almost a thing of the past, this flavour is acceptable, in fact, the very essence of sherry style wines where these acetaldehyde produced flavours and bouquets that are sought after. Yet many wine lovers, rightly, dislike similar tastes in table wines.

Long bottle maturation will eventually see white wines develop pleasant golden to amber/brown colours. People with a long experience evaluating these wines may enjoy them, although most of today's wine lovers prefer the freshness of young or current vintage whites. This change in public opinion has brought favourable changes to winemaking philosophies in Spain and Italy.

FORTIFIED WINES

Fortified wines are those with added alcohol, the popular styles being sherry, port, vermouth, marsala and the incredible Australian liqueur muscats and tokays from the Rutherglen region of Victoria.

Sherry—Fino

Spanish styles of sherry range from extremely dry to very sweet, although each style is made from 'white' grapes; all start with juice colours similar to lemon juice. The popular dry manzanilla and fino styles are bottled early after limited barrel and flor yeast contact, then consumed as young wines minus any oxidative colouring. They could best be described as pale fresh straw colour. Fino, in fact, means fine.

Sherry—Amontillado

Amontillado is fino that has been kept in barrels for ten years plus allowing it to become slowly oxidised and develop fuller viscosity and flavour through evaporation. This process brings about a golden, pale tan (old gold) colour and adds considerable complexity to the style.

Sherry—Cream

The sweeter, British cream styles are handled quite differently. Very ripe bunches of grapes are laid on mats in the hot sun to dehydrate, then after fermentation the highly sugary concentrate is left for years in barrel to darken and thicken; they are extremely luscious.

Port

On the other hand, the port styles of vintage, ruby and tawny are made from red/black grapes—the style name is indicated by the colour. All ports start out almost crimson in colour when placed in barrels for maturation. Between one and two years the vintage ports are placed in impervious glass bottles so that 15-20 years later they still retain their youthful appearance.

Ruby and tawny ports are left in barrels until sufficient colour pigments precipitate, giving them their respective colours of ruby or tawny. In the process they pick up some oxidative colour and flavours. The more time tawny ports are left in barrel the more colour pigments fall out and the wine finally becomes a true tawny with no red pigments at all. There comes a time in the evolution process when the sherries, made from white wines, have picked up more oxidative colour and are darker than ports.

Sherry-styles

Ruby & tawny Port

31

APPEARANCE—ALL TABLE WINES

USEFUL DESCRIPTIONS

Positive	Negative
Clear	Dull
Bright	Cloudy
Star bright	Precipitated
Brilliant	Gassy (table wines)

Sparkling Wines   bubble size — quantity, rate, duration.

COLOURFUL DESCRIPTIONS

White	Red	Sparkling Wines
Colourless	Pink	Same as white table wine
Very light straw	Rosé	Blanc de noir (white from red)
Light straw	Light or purplish red	Various shades of salmon
Straw/green	Dark/deep red	Eye of the Partridge
Fresh straw	Tawny/brick red	Bronze-coppery
Medium yellow/straw		
Light gold		
Gold		
Rich/Deep Gold		

SIGHT RECORD

These sheets have been designed to cater for *all* wine styles, in which case some material will be irrelevant to individual styles. The information below is what you will find on the *Right Column* of the Wine Evaluation Record (score sheet).

Prior to Assessment

Appearance: Brilliant, star-bright, bright, clear, dull, cloudy, precipitated.

Colour: Colourless, very light/light/straw, straw green, light/medium/dark gold. Blushing pink, rose, light/purplish/medium/dark/tawny/brick red.

Saturation: Light, medium, deep.

Bubbles: Spritzig, size, quantity, rate, duration.

WINE DETAILS		SIGHT 4 max	AROMA/ BOUQUET 6 max	IN MOUTH 6 max	AFTER FLAVOUR 2 max	OVERALL 2 max	TOTAL 20 max
1	Vintage '01 Cullen Variety Chardonnay Region Margaret River	4					
		Comments	Light gold colour–brilliant appearance,				
2	Vintage '01 Bouchard Pere Variety Chardonnay Region Le Montrachet	3.5					
		Comments	Light straw colour–bright appearance,				
3	Vintage '01 Robert Mondavi Variety Chardonnay Region Napa CA	3.75					
		Comments	Golden colour–appearance clear.				
4	Vintage '01 Hamilton Russell Variety Chardonnay Region Walker Bay, S.Africa	4					
		Comments	Medium straw colour–brilliant appearance;				
5	Vintage '01 Floating Mtn Variety Chardonnay Region Waipara NZ	4					
		Comments	Light golden colour–appearance star-bright.				

Wine evaluation record sheet (WER) showing SIGHT scores and comments

Figure 13

4 points	Excellent	Brilliant with outstanding characteristic colour
3 points	Good	Bright with characteristic colour
2 points	Average	Clear, without obvious faults.
1 point	Poor	Dull or slightly off-colour
0 points	Objectionable	Cloudy and off-colour

Please use fractions, i.e. ½ points or decimal points. Very few wines should score less than three points.

It is an absolute must that as you go through each of the exercises, that you *practice your vocabulary*—preferably with another person—for the given wine or solution. Use the words provided, or add any that are easily understood—and portable.

Very important information

In this way you will quickly learn about each component, in addition you will build up a worthwhile vocabulary that can be understood anywhere. Please avoid the use of words with parochial meanings.

GLOSSARY OF SIGHT—COLOUR WORDS

Anthocyanins

Anthocyanins are flavonoids, water-soluble plant pigments which provide most of the red, pink and blue colours in plants, fruits and flowers.

Clarity

Clearness—opposite to turbid.

Extraction

Extraction is what makes red wine different to white wine. Extraction during fermentation produces the colour pigments, tannins and aromatic substances.

Flavonoid

A group of aromatic, oxygen-containing heterocyclic pigments widely distributed among higher plants. They constitute most of the yellow, red and blue colours in flowers and fruits. Anthocyanin is one of the four possible flavonoid sub-groups.

Flavour

Flavour is a combination of aroma, taste, and touch (temperature and texture).

Must

Crushed grapes, or juice, until the end of fermentation, when it becomes wine.

Opalescence

A milky iridescence.

Oxidation

Change in wine or food caused by exposure to air.

Oxidation-Reduction Reactions

Oxidation and reduction always occur simultaneously with the transfer of electrons. The substances that gain and lose electrons are referred to respectively as the oxidising and reducing agents.

Phenolics

Phenolics are basically, the colour pigments (anthocyanins) and tannins, that provide astringency.

Pigments

Colouring matter.

Figure 14

These three wines all started life the colour of lemon juice. Note the difference.

Left: Spatlese; Centre: Auslese. Right: Rutherglen Muscat. With age the lemon juice colour has tanned through the process of oxidation.

(Glasses have been cut in half, lengthwise, to avoid glare).

Figure 15

Left: Classic Australian Syrah, six years old. Note strong colour extending to edge of liquid—this indicates that the wine has a lot of life

Centre: Classic California 'Meritage' blend (Bordeaux grapes), 8 years old, just starting to show hints of brown on meniscus. Still very good for long ageing

Right: 20-year-old SouthAfrican Cabernet. Long ago it lost its red, purple, blue colours that have now been replaced by the tannin colours. However, still showing class with colour still touching the meniscus.

(Glasses have been cut in half, lengthwise, to avoid glare).

Figure 16

WHITE #1 Amontillado sherry average age 10-15 years

Shows colour development by oxidation. As a young wine this was lemon juice colour.

Now starts as straw colour at the rim, extending through gold to amber at the eye of the wine.

Figure 17

WHITE #3 An aged Oloroso exceeding 20 years

Wine made from white grapes, highlights colour solely from oxidation. In appearance it is almost identical to a mature tawny port, maybe has more colour!

Figure 18

WHITE #2 A top New Zealand Riesling—10 years old

No rim colour, overall a pale lemon-straw colour. Glistening with brightness of low pH and high acidity. Long term cellaring. Colour and complexity will develop with bottle evolution.

Two "white" wines

Figure 19

WHITE #4 A unique Australian Muscat

Surely points out the folly of calling wines 'white'! Made from Muscat grapes, juice was lemon-coloured; this wine is liqueured in barrels (not topped-up) allowing intense concentration. Blend contains wines ranging from 10-80 years old. Exquisite dessert wine, colour and flavour complex in the extreme

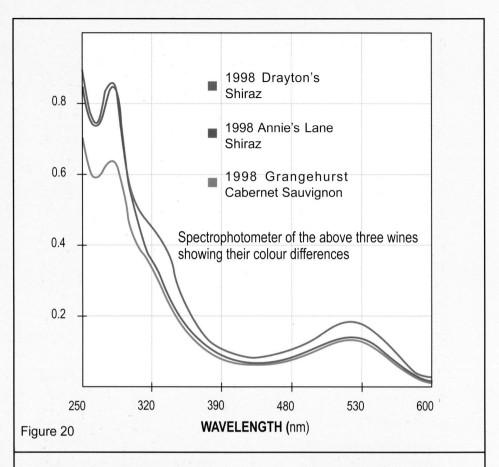

0.8

0.6

0.4

0.2

■ 1998 Drayton's Shiraz

■ 1998 Annie's Lane Shiraz

■ 1998 Grangehurst Cabernet Sauvignon

Spectrophotometer of the above three wines showing their colour differences

250   320   390   480   530   600

Figure 20   **WAVELENGTH (nm)**

RIGHT HAND COLUMN OF YOUR WINE EVALUATION RECORD (WER)

Follow the right hand column of your WER carefully and you will, in a short time, know more about wine (for you) than anyone alive.

But, like all instructions, they must be followed at all times—not just as a convenience.

Note the sections 1. PRIOR TO IN-MOUTH and 2. IN-MOUTH and how they are broken-up to other sections; olfactory and gustation are covered in the following chapters.

For now, just concentrate on the SIGHT chapter. Record your impressions of *Appearance* and *Colour* and then *Chroma/Saturation.*

You can lift your skills way-up, and simply, by using this chart when seriously evaluating wine.

PRIOR TO IN-MOUTH

1. SIGHT
Appearance: Brilliant, star bright, bright, clear, dull, cloudy, precipitated.
Colour: Colourless, very light/light/straw/ straw green,light/medium/dark gold Pink, rose, light/purplish/medium/ dark/tawny/brick red

Saturation: Light, medium, deep

2. OLFACTORY
Aroma: Fruity, floral, spicy, vegetative, earthy.
Intensity: 1, 2, 3, 4, 5, 6, 7, 8, 9, 10
Bouquet: Clean, fresh, dirty, H_2S, mercaptans), yeast, oak, SO_2 (no irritation)
Intensity: -5, 4, 3, 2, 1, 0 +1, 2, 3, 4, 5

IN-MOUTH

3. GUSTATORY
Viscosity: Watery, thin, medium, full-bodied
Taste: Sugar, bitter, acid, salt, umami, flavour
Olfactory Earthy, fruity, floral, umami, herbaceous, woody, sweet, complex.
Tactile: Temperature, texture, irritation, gas, viscosity
Length: Long. meduium, short
After-flavour: Excellent, good, OK, none

Attention to detail is paramount at a wine evaluation; the correct glasses, light grey table cothes or place mats, water for rinsing glasses and mouths—and appropriate lighting.

Here you can see the incandescent lights at the rear, bright natural light coming from the left and diffused natural light from the front.

Although looking at the same objects, each person is looking at something entirely different because of the light sources.

Figure 21
Daylight

Figure 22
Daylight Fluorescent

These four photographs were taken with the same film at the correct exposure but under four different light sources.

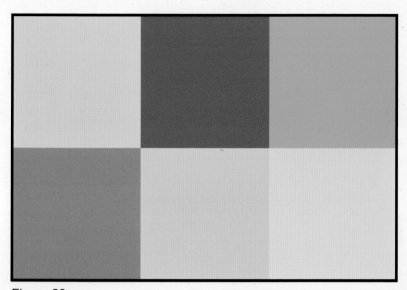

Figure 23

Incandescent

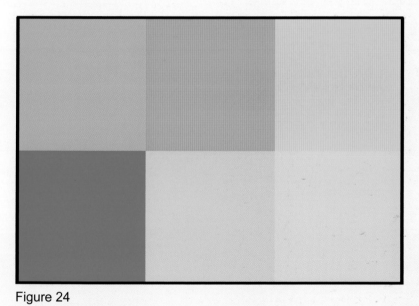

Figure 24

Ordinary fluorescent

Photos by Ernest Laidlaw BA AIAP

SIGHT MADE EASY

1. A bright colour, for example, is not a pleasant bonus in wine that is otherwise good or bad, it is necessarily part of its quality.

2. Our language reflects our limitations. The Eskimos are reputed to have over 40 words for snow reflecting the extraordinary ability to discriminate within the dominant colour of their culture, whereas dwellers in more temperate regions are severely limited in their perception and language.

3. People with normal colour vision will match colours, and mixtures of colours, in a very similar way. Normal eyes can match a spectrum yellow by a suitable mixture of spectrum red and spectrum green. The colour defective require much more green, or red, depending on the nature of their ailment-in the red/green mix to match the spectrum yellow. This is a fairly severe handicap when assessing red and ageing white table wines.

4. The primary source of wine colour comes from the grape skins; the second source is oxidation. Oxidation is the brown discolouration that appears when we cut an apple or pear (and so many other fruits and vegetables). Grape juice and wine suffer the same browning when exposed to uncontrolled oxygen.

5. Any colour can be described by making use of three attributes, hue, saturation and chroma. These are widely used in the textile, dyestuffs or paint industries.

6. Hue is the red, yellow, green and blue (or intermediate between adjacent pairs of these) tints that comprise our wine colour. Black, white and neutral grey have no hue.

7. In simple terms, turbidity is the opposite of clarity. It is particulate matter, the material that causes haze or turbidity and protects microbes from the killing action of disinfectants that gives us bacterial spoilage.

8. What are tears and legs? The answer comes in two parts—first is the difference in surface tension between water and alcohol, the second is the viscosity of the wines, the differential evaporation of alcohol, sugar and glycerols combining with the wine. All in all, legs and tears are best kept out of wine talk; most wine people find it boring.

9. The amazing phenomenon of flair and metamerism, combined with the known facts that the perception of colour varies from one person to another, and that we don't have an accepted standard light source for wine appraisal, leads us to all sorts of conjecture. While the one constant attribute of wine colour is the wine itself, the other two elements of colour perception—the source of illumination—and the perceiver—are changing with each appraisal.

10. Now, let us look at the appearance of the wine, starting with the surface, followed by the brightness. Record your observations on a score sheet, preferably the one recommended on page 33. This will ensure that you don't skip any of the fundamentals.

    Proceed with a preliminary olfactory sniff and then a quick 'in mouth' appraisal, solely for the purpose of confirming your visual observations. Having smelled, felt and tasted the wine, go back to the visual aspects and check the relationship of colour-viscosity, colour-acidity, colour-nose, colour-flavour and colour-length of after-flavour.

    Having carefully chosen the best available glassware (see pages 47–49) and the best available lighting, we now need an area devoid of strong colours that could reflect or conflict with the wine colours. White beneath and around the glass is good, light grey or a buff colour is better—but in most instances it is sufficient to have a white tablecloth.

11. There are four positions from which wine colour can be examined:

    a) Try to make evaluations as the wine is poured from the bottle while it is between bottle and glass—looking at the wine as it's poured, or as it splashes in the glass. This is not easy and it requires a lot of concentration. Try this every time you see wine poured, a good background of light grey/buff helps.

    b) The most common everyday appraisal is when the glass of wine sits on the table and is viewed obliquely against a favourable background.

    c) For critical analysis, rotate the glass quickly, swirling the wine so that it climbs up the side of the glass, and look through the swirling wine. This will reveal any giveaway brown signs of premature ageing. (At the same time the swirling wine coats the total surface of the glass readying it for the olfactory appraisal.)

    d) Tilt the glass away from you so that a tongue of wine reaches the very rim of the glass. For red wine appraisal, I use a champagne flute. A flute allows for a long tongue—and this is what must be examined. Here the heart and soul of wine colour is exposed.

12. First, look for the purity of colour—has a young red or white wine any of the spoilt factors that were discussed on pages 19–20. Then check to see that there is no watery rim around the edges, or on the tip of the tongue. Quality red wines with cellaring potential will have pure colour right to the meniscus—the very tip of the tongue and along the sides. Young white wines should be free of any signs of oxidation.

13. Saturation of colour is our next concern as this will indicate the body or viscosity of the wine. If in doubt, go back and check page 18.

Proceed with a preliminary olfactory and then a quick 'in mouth' appraisal, solely for the purpose of confirming your visual observations. Look at the wine, think about each of these factors and next time you are speaking to a winemaker (or similarly trained person) discuss your findings.

It is an absolute must that as you go through each of the exercises, that you practice your vocabulary—preferably with another person—for the given wine or solution. Use the words provided, or add any that are easily understood and portable.

In this way you will quickly learn about each component, in addition you will build up a worthwhile vocabulary that can be understood anywhere. Please avoid the use of words with parochial meanings.

SIGHT SUMMARY

- Do not rush into sight appraisal any more than you would bypass the visual aspects of food presentation.

- Take a thorough and methodical approach, bearing in mind that the winemaker has taken at least two years to get a red wine in the bottle; please don't dismiss it in a few seconds.

- Ensure that the lighting and ambience are the best available.

- Use only well shaped sparkling clean glassware.

- Carefully separate your appraisal of colour from appearance.

- The two sources of colour are grape skins and oxidation—refer to page 15 and 16.

- Tip the glass away from you so that a long 'tongue' exposes the body and soul of the wine. Practice reading the meniscus!

WHAT DID YOU LEARN FROM THIS CHAPTER?

1. What is needed to form an image? (page 22)
2. How many colour discriminations can the eye perceive? (page 12)
3. How important is colour in wine evaluation?
4. Explain the *origins* of colour in red wine? (page 15)
5. What part of evaluation does *clarity* cover? (page 19)
6. What is *metamerism?* (page 22)
7. What is daylight and can it be reproduced by artificial light? (page 26)
8. Explain the visual examination of red wine. (page 25)
9. What words are used to describe the colours of white wine? (page 32)
10. What role do *phenolics* play in wine.(page 15)

CHAPTER 3

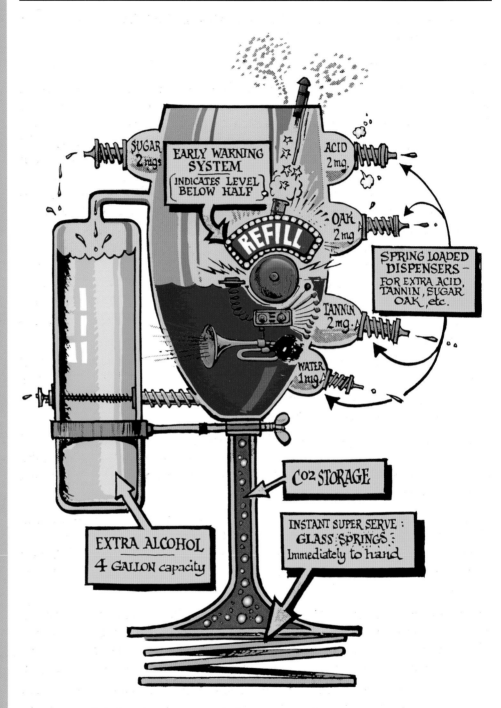

Rigby-Young Wine Tasting Glass Mark 2

GLASSWARE

What glassware, or stemware as they are called in the USA, should be used for wine appraisal?

Shape and Colour

If you have a set of those ornate purple, blue or green glasses that a friend gave you for a wedding present, rush out right now and smash them; take the saucer shaped 'champagne' glasses with you and give them a smashing time also. (If you have a favourite aunt who doesn't approve of waste, make a big hit by presenting them to her; they are no use for wine evaluation or enjoyment.) Coloured glasses are nothing more than a European fad to hide the oxidised colour of poor quality wine and the Hollywood-promoted champagne saucers, allegedly moulded from Marie Antoinette's bosom, are useful only for seafood cocktails or chocolate mousse.

Visually, wine is all about beautiful colours—purples, blues, reds of a fine red wine and brilliant straw to golden colours of a white wine. Only clear glass will reveal this beauty—expensive cut glass adds nothing and as a general rule bulky glasses are poorly balanced. An additional interesting point is that not only are cut lead crystal glasses bulky and heavy, but it is also possible that they are unhealthy.*

Cut lead crystal

The 'feel' of a glass can make people comfortable or otherwise at a meal. And those funny looking V or ice cream cone-shaped martini glasses are worthless for anything other than martinis. A wineglass should taper in at the top—not taper outwards. However tulip shaped glasses are commendable.

What's the answer? I go along with the American idea of big glasses, and good, economically priced glasses are readily available in US stores. At the University of Western Sydney (UWS) classes we use an Italian glass known as Reserva Calici 55 ml Bordeaux.

There is every reason to believe that big glasses make for better visual and olfactory appraisal. Even though small IOC glasses are widely used in Australia, small glasses definitely limit the full scope of appraisal. Under no conditions should non-glassware be considered for dining or serious evaluation.

The answer

Customs authorities in most countries enforce health regulations on imported goods. In some countries infra-red lighting is used to detect the lead content of crystal glassware and bone china. Samples are rejected depending on the intensity of blue coloring that shows in the glass or china while under the light.

In these days of no asbestos, lead-free fuel, salt-free foods and non-usage of many other products once considered normal or standard, one might ponder any benefits of using lead crystal glasses.

Flutes

The reasons I find the champagne flute ideal are:

- The size of an object is the most generally accepted factor in seeing.

   Which F is the easiest to see and evaluate—F or ꜰ?

- The flute allows for a long 'tongue' when the glass is tilted forward bringing the wine to the very rim of the glass. What to expect in the tongue of the wine is fully covered in the sight/colour chapter.

- The larger the surface area of glass the better for olfactory appraisal. The volume of odour available for olfactory appraisal is directly related to the surface area of the glass wetted by wine.

Sparkling Clean

Whatever glass you choose, sparkling cleanliness is the keynote. Wherever possible, avoid the use of detergents in glass washing as this causes a film on the glass. This is disastrous for sparkling wines which just won't bubble. Instead, wash glasses in hot water with dish-washing machine powder.

On one occasion we were setting up for a dinner at which the principal guest was the New Zealand Prime Minister and, on testing the champagne flutes, we found that the wine wouldn't sparkle in the glasses. This necessitated the quick purchase of some very fine wet and dry sandpaper and by rotating this in the glasses we were able to remove the residual detergent and return the glasses to a useful state.

Make sure that your white wines aren't so cold that they frost up the outside of the glass. Condensation is hard to see through, somewhat similar to looking through opaque glass, and this will have a marked effect on your ability to distinguish between brilliant, bright and clear.

Whatever glass you decide on, fill it only from a quarter to a third, about 30 to 40 ml or 1 to 2 ounces. The worst thing for evaluation is too much wine in the glass.

OK Glasses

Good Glasses

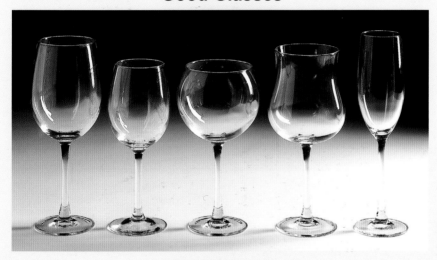

Ideal Glass*

Clear thin glass

Maximum—
level for drinking

Sufficient—
level for evaluation

Tulip Shaped Tapered
Neck: stops swirling
splash

Large Bowl: for
maximum surface area

*Pictured: Vindel™

CHAPTER 4

The sense of smell—the action of smelling, from the Latin—olfacere, to smell

Oh, dear me—not Cabernet—AGAIN!

SMELL—OLFACTION

If the international wine lover has one common failing it is the enthusiastic desire to rush the wine into the mouth and start tasting. This act bypasses two of the more important senses—smell and sight.

Now, there's nothing wrong with rushing the wine into the mouth if one is simply in search of a drink. But, as we are discussing the sensory appraisal of wine, it's vitally important that we use some of our other senses before getting on with the business of drinking.

ANALYSIS OF SMELLY COMPOUNDS

Many researchers around the world have long been interested in the nature of odoriferous substances or 'chemoreception'. These substances are usually volatile, those which easily evaporate to form a vapour or gas phase. The word 'volatile' comes from the Latin *volare*—to fly. Other Latin descriptive words are volatilis—winged, swift, fleeting, and volaticus—winged, fleeting, inconstant. Due to the fleeting, inconstant nature of gases and vapours, it was difficult to analyse and study these compounds until the invention only 45 years ago, of the gas chromatograph (GC).

Inconsistent nature of gases

The GC is an instrument capable of separating complex mixtures of volatile substances (those which pass off easily in the form of a vapour, i.e. gaseous, or in the gas phase). Once an aroma can be separated into its various components, its chemistry can be studied. The process of separation is not easy, mainly because so much of smell is elusive. Wine, for example, may give off several hundred volatile compounds that together may still represent only a few parts per million of weight. This volatile fraction, in turn, may contain only a few compounds that are odoriferous enough to make a contribution to the aroma and, more often than not, these are present in only trace amounts.

Volatile fractions

There are some added complications in detecting the aromas of wine: firstly, of the about approximately 4000 compounds so far detected in wine, only about 500 cause aromas. Secondly, some of the odiferous compounds bound tightly to sugar molecules in grapes and fresh wine render them inactive until natural ageing processes and the wine's acidity slowly release the aromas. Some examples of these aromas give *honey, tobacco, chocolate* and *dried fig* aromas in aged Merlot and Cabernet wines.

Mechanised nose

It is said that only seven of 92 basic chemical elements are odoriferous; flourine, chlorine, bromine, iodine, oxygen (as ozone), phosphorus and arsenic. Most of what we perceive as smells come from volatile chemical compounds. The modern gas chromatograph equipped with capillary columns, is a mechanized version of the human nose; it can separate 200–400 compounds from one particular wine or foodstuff. The chemist sniffs the effluent gases from the GC at frequent intervals and records observations.

The detection of volatile compounds by gas chromatography involves three steps: 1. Separation of the smelly mixture into individual components by the gas chromatograph (GC) itself 2. Detection of these separated components by some process fitted to the chromatograph (called the 'detector') and 3. Identification of the chemical nature of the components of interest.

In comparison with a machine such as the GC, our nose can separate and detect individual components of a smelly mixture simultaneously, then send a signal to the brain, which in turn analyses this response immediately and causes us to act in some appropriate manner. This process is described in more detail later in the chapter.

The gas chromatograph (GC) or, more accurately a gas-liquid chromatograph (GLC) contains a fine, hollow capillary tube up to 300 metres long made from fused silica glass. It contains a sticky, waxy liquid phase firmly bonded to the inner surface of the tube. This is the 'liquid' of the formal name of the apparatus. This tube is usually coiled up like a tiny hose and placed in an oven. Various control systems can program the rate of heating so that conditions can be tuned to the particular requirements of the sample being analysed.

Vapourised components

When the sample (such as a particular wine) is to be analysed, a tiny amount (around 2 micro-millilitres—two millionth of a millilitre) is injected in a heated area at the top of the capillary column so that all the volatile components are vapourised. This vapour is wafted through the column on a stream of an unreactive gas such as helium or nitrogen. This is the 'gas' in the name of the method—gas chromatography. The gas pressure and flow rate are also programmed, along with the oven temperature mentioned above, so as to optimise the conditions to suit each particular sample.

The *chromatography* from the name of the method refers to what happens next. It is a general name for separation of components, and the name comes from the original technique of separating coloured substances. Each different compound in our volatilized wine mixture will evaporate at a different temperature, and will also have a different attraction for the liquid layer on the inside of the capillary. By balancing the oven temperature and gas flow rate, we can set conditions so that each compound will emerge from the other end at a different time.

However, we won't know this unless we have some type of detector on the end of the capillary column, and some way of recording what is detected. There is a wide variety of detectors that are commonly used, each relying on a different property of the effluent compounds. Some detect a change in current when a compound passes through the detector (see E-noses on page 75); some cause a chemical reaction with particular classes of compound, and some rely on biological properties—such as a person sniffing the effluent gases and making a recording when they smell something interesting.

When strong odours are present they are described in simple terms such as *green grass, oniony, rose-like*. These are recorded on tape and their position marked on the chart of the GC. Thus the peaks that correspond with strong odours are readily located and the compounds that make them are pinpointed for further study. If 10 compounds in the GC, for example, have been humanly identified with 'green grass', they are then further separated to see what chemical features they have in common.

Describing odours

COMPARISON BETWEEN FID
AND DETECTION BY HUMAN NOSE (AROMAGRAM)

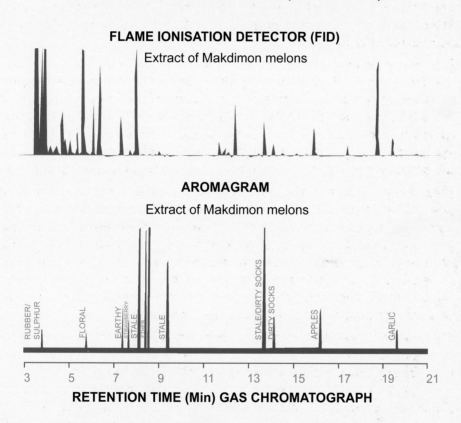

FLAME IONISATION DETECTOR (FID)
Extract of Makdimon melons

AROMAGRAM
Extract of Makdimon melons

RETENTION TIME (Min) GAS CHROMATOGRAPH

Note that some peaks, representing components of the melon extract, that are present in the FID are not detected by the human nose, whereas some components that are strongly odiferous show very small peaks when detected electronically. Also note the colourful terms used to describe the individual odours of the mixture by the person who prepared the aromagram.

Unable to identify

While the GC effectively separates volatile substances it is unable to identify them. Also, humans are not very good at naming or remembering odours (as will be discussed later in the chapter). Fortunately there are now more objective means of identifying the chemical nature of the compounds, This task is performed by such instruments as a mass spectrometer (MS) and it is fortunate that means were found to which can be linked these two instruments to form a powerful research tool—the GC-MS.

Formation of esters

$$CH_3CH_2OH \quad + \quad CH_3C{\underset{OH}{\overset{O}{\vphantom{|}}}} \quad \longrightarrow \quad CH_3CH_2-O-\underset{O}{\overset{}{C}}-CH_3 \quad + \quad H_2O$$

from ethanol | from acetic acid

Ethanol	Acetic acid	Ethyl acetetate	Water
(an	(an organic acid)	(an ester)	

Stereo chemistry

Since every compound produces characteristic patterns of ions (electrically charged atoms) in its mass spectrum, that spectrum, for practical purposes, may be regarded as its fingerprint and can be identified in the GC-MS.

In the initial studies of the flavour of green peas, for example, the human nose acting in conjunction with the GC was used to recognize three compounds with intense odours. Subsequent studies over four years, during which time only a few micrograms of each material could be extracted, showed that the three were structurally related.

Here there was no problem of stereoisomers (two substances which may have the same basic structure but have different stereochemistry—the actual arrangement of atoms in space) but the chemical instability of the compounds prevented the collection of structural information by micro chemical transformations.

Structures were predicted from their mass spectra, and synthetic studies eventually gave the structures of the natural materials. Their structures differ in only one grouping, which greatly influences the aroma of the compound.

Compound (A)   Compound (B)

A & B compounds found in the Cabernets, Merlot and Sauvignon.

Compound (C)   Compound (D)

From a wine lover's point of view this has broken new ground, as we had not known what gave certain wines their particular fragrances. Compounds A and B with the iso propyl and sec-butyl groups have similar odours, akin to freshly opened green pea shells, but compound C with the iso-butyl group is quite different. Its aroma is characteristic of green peppers or capsicums; similar aromas are found in the Cabernets and Merlot.

These compounds are amongst the most odoriferous known and are present in fresh green peas in extremely small amounts on the order of one part in 100,000 million! Recently these compounds have been shown to be present in varying small amounts in many other raw vegetables, including green beans, broad beans, lettuce, spinach, carrot and beetroot. They are now believed to occur commonly in minute amounts in many green plants, and may also be in wines.

Very smelly

Earthy

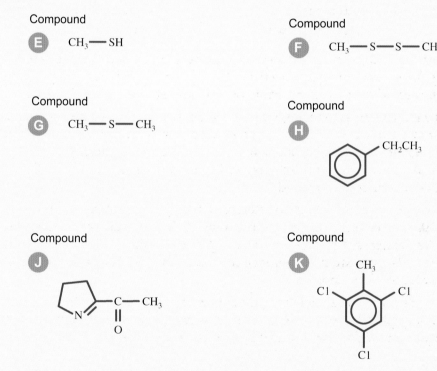

Compound

E $CH_3 — SH$

Compound

F $CH_3 — S — S — CH_3$

Compound

G $CH_3 — S — CH_3$

Compound

H

Compound

J

Compound

K

In beetroot, another highly odoriferous compound was detected. This substance, which has a strong 'earthy' odour was subsequently identified as geosmin, compound D, a known compound, which is the main aroma component of freshly turned earth. It is known to be produced by some classes of micro organisms in soils and in water catchments where it imparts an earthy quality to the water, and, no doubt, is responsible for the many wines given an 'earthy' classification.

Beetroot

In the future, it will be refreshing to attend wine tastings and hear references to the pyrazines and such terms as isopropyl, secbutyl, isobutyl, and geosmin in addition to the few compounds now recognised—diacetyl (dimethyl diketone), hydrogen sulphide (H_2S) and sulphur dioxide (SO_2), instead of the non specific adjectives that the 'in-set' use to bully their friends.

Chemical nomenclature

And won't the earthy smell of geosmin be a nice piece of one upmanship for the wine and food set? Although there is still the danger of becoming unfashionable, as the chemical nomenclature is changing and the terms 'sec' and 'iso' are replaced by a numbering system under the strict systematic rules for naming organic compounds, and there are several names for diacetyl, including dimethyl diketone and 2,3-butanedione. So with this knowledge, one can choose the level of one-upmanship one desires to use.

Individual components

For those with a penchant for the chemical structure of wine and food, this is how these chemicals are constructed.

Some unusual compounds are present in tiny amounts in the wine. In large amounts these sometimes smell foul—but when present in combination with the other aromas in the wine, they may be very important in giving the individual characteristics to each particular bottle of wine. The chemical structures of methyl mercaptan (or methanethiol)—burning rubber (E); dimethyl disulphide—onion (F); dimethyl sulphide—asparagus (G); and 4-ethylphenol—horse blankets (H) are shown on page 55.

Bad smells

Other compounds in wine arise from the strain of yeast used, the soil or weather conditions present when grapes are grown and ripened, and the oak casks used during the fermentation process.

Then there are the truly 'bad' smells that are not desirable, even in tiny quantities (as shown in the table). One of these is 2-acetyl-1-pyrroline (J), which smells like mouse urine and has a long-lasting after-flavour. Another is the aroma of tainted cork, which is one of the five most potent aromas to humans. Its chemical name is 2,4,6-trichloroanisole or TCA (K), and it can be formed by the washing of corks with chlorine bleaches is the most common source. Many problems also come from wine barrels and chlorine used in cleaning winery floors and equipment.

ADDITIONAL USES FOR ANALYSIS TECHNIQUES

The coupling of the gas chromatograph to the mass spectrometer (MS) was a giant step in the identification of components responsible for the aroma of wine and food flavours. The developments (*circa* 1970) of polymers (compounds of high molecular weight) capable of retaining the volatile organic compounds with the exclusion of water (or alcohol) have been an equally large step in the isolation and concentration of aroma substances.

Classical techniques

Prior to this development, classical techniques involving distillation, followed usually by solvent extraction, then concentration by evaporation of solvent were employed. Such a procedure frequently led to the destruction of sensitive but highly important aroma compounds.

The new collection techniques, when coupled to the instrumental power of the GS-MS, has allowed the research worker to undertake tasks previously considered impossible. Some examples include studies of the variation of flavour components between individual single fruits, the monitoring of changes taking place during fruit ripening, and the identification of differences in meat flavours produced by feeding animals on different diets or by the use of different slaughtering techniques.

Because of these successes, the techniques have been used to study such elusive problems as the chemicals responsible for photochemical smog, insect and animal pheromones and human metabolic disorders as evidenced by the excretion of novel metabolites.

Only in recent years has it been possible to identify wines in the laboratory made from individual grape varieties; DNA has taken over this role. It is also interesting to note that routine laboratory analysis (other than by spectrophotometer) cannot, as yet, make any distinction between a great and an ordinary wine.

CHEMISTRY OF SMELL

The most abundant volatiles of wine are aldehydes, alcohols and esters. Briefly, aldehydes are derivatives of alcohol. (see table page 74.)

Aldehydes

Many aldehydes have low 'odour thresholds' for humans, meaning they can be detected in very small quantities. This means they may be very important in determining characteristic smells (such as hexanal in fresh apples and octanal and decanal in citrus juices).

Some of them are also known to be involved in natural 'wound response' compounds in plants. These compounds have recently been shown to be important in the communication between plants and animals (for example, in attracting or repelling pollinators, predators or beneficial insects) and also in plant-plant interactions, where they may help plant communities initiate an immune-like series of responses to the wound. Some of them are also anti-microbial compounds that stop infection in the wound.

Plants and animals

Many aldehydes are also important in animal communication as insect pheromones, and perhaps also in the complex mixtures that make up animal pheromones.

An interesting example of a commercially important oderiferous aldehyde is the perfume Chanel No.5, which was the first perfume to use synthetic compounds (more readily and cheaply available than the natural oils). One of these was the synthetic aldehyde 2-methylundecanal (L). When alcohols are oxidized they occupy an intermediate position between primary alcohols and acids which are formed on further oxidation. Vanillin in oak is an aldehyde. It is vanillin extracted from the barrel staves during barrel maturation that provides the familiar vanilla smell that many wine lovers recognize as oak in wine.

Vanillin

Smell exercise #1 Cut an apple in half, wrap one half in plastic wrap and cut the remaining half into segments. Smell freshly cut segments, then allow to go brown (oxidize) for 30 minutes or more. The fresh smell of apple will be replaced by the smell of aldehyde. Bring out your wrapped half, cut it into segments and smell the oxidized and fresh segments sides separately.

Smell Exercise #1

What has happened here is that the odour and colour change and this is due to oxidation—but to other than simple alcohol to aldehyde reaction.

57

Just for the record, more than 45 odoriferous compounds have been isolated that contribute to the aroma of an apple. When we talk about the smell of an apple, what are we talking about? Cooking changes some of these odoriferous compounds—does an apple pie or apple juice really smell like a freshly cut apple?

Oxidation of wine can lead to the production of compounds such as aldehydes and acetic acid (vinegar). As you will notice, the presence of aldehydes will greatly change the natural aromatic character of wine, or apples. (In small amounts, oxidation can also be a complexing factor; in more than small amounts it is definitely a negative factor.)

Some of these changes may cause undesirable odours and flavours. The word 'vinegar' comes from the French words 'vin—wine' and 'aigre—a fever or illness'. Hence *vin-aigre* means *diseased wine*. However, some more complex oxidative changes may be part of the natural ageing processes that contribute to the individual character of each wine.

The chemical relationship between alcohols, aldehydes, organic acids (such as vinegar) and esters is shown in the diagram below.

Alcohols

Alcohols occur widely in nature, and are present in simple 'fresh' aromas as well as more complex aromas such as volatile or essential oils. By way of interest, raspberries and strawberries contain at least seven different alcohols; bananas seven (five are the same as strawberries); oranges about 15, and wine contains more than 15 alcohols.

Wine to vinegar (alcohol to aldehyde to organic acid):

$$CH_3CH_2OH \xrightarrow[\text{micro-organisms}]{\text{oxidation}} CH_3C\!\!\begin{array}{c}{}^{\displaystyle O}\\{}_{\displaystyle H}\end{array} \xrightarrow[\text{in air (O}_2\text{)}]{\text{oxidation}} CH_3C\!\!\begin{array}{c}{}^{\displaystyle O}\\{}_{\displaystyle OH}\end{array}$$

ethanol	ethanal	ethanoic acid
(ethyl alcohol)	(acetaldehyde)	(acetic acid, vinegar)

$$CH_3CH_2OH + CH_3C\!\!\begin{array}{c}{}^{\displaystyle O}\\{}_{\displaystyle OH}\end{array} \longrightarrow CH_3CH_2\!-\!O\!-\!\underset{\underset{O}{\|}}{C}\!-\!CH_3 + H_2O$$

Fusel oils are higher alcohols that contribute to mouth feel. Smoothness is the fusel oil characteristic most familiar to the brandy sipper. When alcohols are oxidised, they first produce aldehydes. In the formation of vinegar, this first step is mediated by some undesirable micro-organisms present in the wine barrel. Aldehydes are easily oxidised in a small amount of air to organic (carboxylic) acids (of which acetic acid, vinegar, is a simple example).

Not all aldehydes are undesirable, and not all of them are easily oxidised—for example vanillin in oak is an aldehyde. It is vanillin extracted from the barrel staves during wine maturation in barrels that provides the familiar vanilla smell that many wine lovers recognize as oak in wine.

Esters

Esters are derived from acids by the exchange of the replaceable hydrogen of the acid for an organic radical; esters of acetic acid are called *acetates*. Esters, aromatic odiferous compounds, are one of the main components monitored by the GC. The several types of esters found in many fruits and in brandy are responsible for the characteristic aroma. Esters, aromatic compounds, aldehydes, also GC tested, are complexing agents that complex the esters.

Many, but not all, esters have pleasant smells that are characteristic of particular fruits. As shown in the diagram, they can be made in the laboratory by heating an alcohol and an organic acid with a small amount of a strong acid. In living organisms, particular enzymes catalyse similar reactions. Esters of acetic acid are called acetates, and many names of esters similarly end in "...ate"- giving an idea of the organic acid from which it was derived.

Important uses for low molecular weight esters such as ethyl acetate and butyl acetate are solvents for lacquers, paints and varnishes. Often these types of smells are associated with 'not good' wine.

Synthetic, low molecular weight, esters are used commercially as the base for artificial food flavours. Some of these are: ethyl formate, an artificial essence constituent in peach, raspberry and rum; ethyl acetate, in apple, pear, strawberry and amyl acetate, in banana and apple.

Therefore, it can be seen that the volatile composition of a large number of fruits is similar, but their ratios and trace amounts of other compounds determine what the mixture smells like; whether it is apples, pears and strawberries or other fruits. As you progress with your wine knowledge, the above principles will explain many wine flavours for you.

Not all esters are pleasant-smelling. Oil of Wintergreen (methyl salicylate) is an ester that is present in common sports massage liniments—it is not likely you would like a large amount of this in your wine, or in your fruit. Aspirin (acetyl salicylic acid) is another ester—one that does not smell at all.

Typical Aromas

With few exceptions, the major portion of wine and grape aromas comes from the internal cells of the berry skin. In only a few varieties does the juice aroma dominate. I'm always fascinated when people talk about the *typical* Cabernet or Chardonnay aroma. There is no such thing as typical, not even within one appellation.

Even in Bordeaux, France, the home of the Cabernets, it is well documented that the Cabernet aromas vary considerably from one vineyard to another. Their further different identification becomes a matter of psychology of smell, cultural background and the resource of language we have to describe it. Let's look at the detail of how our smell mechanism actually works.

Acetates

Living organisms

Trace amounts

Berry skin

HOW DO WE SMELL

Dogs are used for laboratory smell tests because of their legendary prowess in that field; two notable examples being their capacity to detect drugs in closed baggage, and from a mile away smell a bitch on heat—possibly the strongest smell in the dog's world, yet not one perceived by humans.

We believe that the male moth has the same smell ability for a distance of 10 kilometres. These and other animals live mainly by smell, whereas we mere mortals read labels and ask questions rather than use our senses. However, we can smell scatol at one part in four billion—or acetic acid at 40 000 times greater than we are able to taste it.

Humans are little different in their smell physiology from dogs, rats and rabbits. In fact, much of what we know about smell has been learnt from these animals.

Humans & animals

Our smell mechanism is divided into three main parts:

1. The receptors located in the olfactory epithelium at the ~~top~~ rear of the nose.

2. The neuro-transmitters (neurons) that carry the chemically charged message.

3. The central (olfactory) cortex which acts something like a switchboard distributing messages to various parts of the brain for response.

Our response to smell can influence learning, memory, sexual or emotional behaviour. As with taste and sight, each person has a different response to smell. Perfume, by way of example, does all sorts of things to people—why? Is it real, or imagined? And the many reactions to a burning smell from the kitchen are worth noting.

There's no need to rush for the family medical dictionary—just let the brilliant pen of Paul Rigby take you for a tour of what's happening in your head.

Remembering smells

Although the sense of smell seems to evoke memories of emotions in a way that is qualitatively different from our other senses, many researchers have noted that humans find it extremely difficult to either remember smells or to name those that are remembered. It is thought that this is because our sense of smell is one of the most primitive senses, and is associated with the limbic system within the brain—that associated with emotions rather than logic—and 'higher' mental tasks.

In two recent studies, it was found that even wine experts were no more skilled at naming familiar odours than were 'people off the street'. Where the wine buffs excelled, however, was in remembering which odours they had already smelt. The other people were not very good at this task, either. The researchers and wine buffs alike think this is due to the practice the experts have had while they have been training their noses, and while they have been continually working in the area of needing to remember. It is probable that naming odours will never be as easy for humans as describing sights, or remembering smells, no matter how much training they have.

Familiar odours

Smell—and the pain sense

In true wine terms, the act of smelling embraces another sense—the pain or irritation sense—and I continually notice, in many countries, that even keen wine judges completely ignore this sense during olfactory appraisal. While we are smelling wine or food we can actually perceive physical irritation from, amongst other substances, alcohol, CO_2 and SO_2 through the free nerve endings in our nasal cavity.

These are different from the nerves that relay the sense of smell to the brain: they are the formal part of the trigeminal nerve system, which itself is sensitive to touch and pain in the whole facial area. Both alcohol and SO_2 are also 'touch' perceivable in the oral cavity; more about that in the next chapter. In the nasal cavity alcohol tends to irritate the bottom portion of the nose, whereas SO_2 penetrates further-up to irritate and dry the upper portion of the nasal passage. SO_2 is strongly reminiscent of a safety match being lit.

Asthma sufferers should acquaint themselves with the smell of SO_2 which is widely used as a food preservative; and, wherever possible, avoid food or beverages containing SO_2. CO_2, present in sparkling wines and carbonated drinks, gives a pleasant tingling sensation that may enhance the taste and smell of the beverage—although it has no smell of its own.

The most important part of the tactile sense during the olfactory assessment is *temperature*. Even though it is comprehensively covered in a later chapter, it would be impossible to overstress its importance here. Wine that is too cold will have a 'dumb' nose—or no nose at all.

Asthma sufferers

Most alcoholic beverages are consumed at temperatures between 40–70°F (5–20°C) and this low temperature inhibits many of the volatile fragrances. When taken into the mouth and warmed to body temperature by the saliva, the increase of some 50% in temperature (to body temperature) produces far more odourous substances in beverages than are available during the external nasal smelling from the glass.

These odourous substances diffuse by way of the back of the mouth up into the inner regions of the nose, where they encounter the smell receptor area. As mentioned earlier, this receptor area is composed of millions of highly specialized cells that are activated by odourous substances and transmit signals to the brain via the neurons.

Lock and Key Principle

There is a popular theory and one to which I subscribe, that odours and receptors work on a lock and key principle. If you have the right lock (receptor) then the key (odour) will open the door; the smell will register. Some molecules, CO_2 is an example, have a shape that will not stimulate the olfactory receptors and is, thus, odourless. Yet in sparkling wines its *touch* effect is a pleasant sensation. Carbon monoxide (automobile exhaust fumes) is a killer gas simply as it is not perceivable by smell.

Killer gas

Odorous substances must be volatile, and soluble in water or fat so that they can pass through the mucous membrane and 'lock' onto the sensitive receptors. Another requirement for our 'key' is to have a molecular weight between 17 and 300—above or below these optimum figures the substances are less odourous.

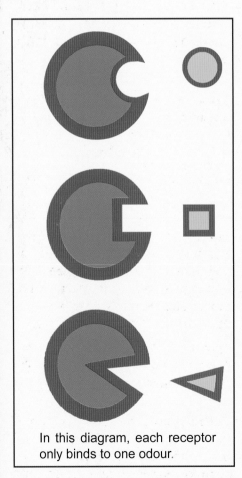

In this diagram, each receptor only binds to one odour.

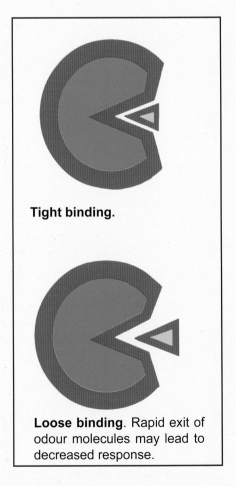

Tight binding.

Loose binding. Rapid exit of odour molecules may lead to decreased response.

In order to have an odour, substances must not only be volatile (as mentioned above), but must also be soluble in oily substances so that they can pass through the mucous membrane that surrounds the receptor cells. Sometimes the odour of a particular compound will depend on how soluble it is in either water or oils (very few are soluble in both).

Molecules also need to be small enough to enter the receptor cells, as larger compounds simply do not 'fit' into the cellular structure. Smaller molecules also tend to be more volatile, and more likely to be odiferous in the first place. In practice, we find that molecules with a molecular weight between 17 and 300 are odiferous. For example, ethanol has a molecular weight of 46, SO_2 is 64, and the green-pea odour shown in structure A earlier in this chapter has a molecular weight of 134.

It is believed that we are all smell 'blind' or merosmic to particular smells—as opposed to not being able to recognise previously unsmelt odours. Each individual has a different level of smell acuity and, I believe, perception to individual fragrances. This is, possibly, borne out by the wide range of men's and women's perfumes.

My own personal 'blind' spots are mint, nuts, oak and pepper and that really limits my red wine repertoire. This selective smell blindness is different to being anosmic—totally unable to smell—which is the fate of only about .01 percent of the population. So it could be said that I have four keys missing from my house of locks. Most of us have some merosmic problem.

Anosmia	temporary or permanent loss of smell
Autosmia	smell perceived when there is no stimulant
Cacosmia	consistently perceive unpleasant smells
Hyperosmia	excessive sensitivity—due to poor health
Merosmia	inability to smell certain aromas
Parosmia	indistinct perception

It was previously mentioned that women are more colour perceptive—the bad news for the male ego is that women are also more smell perceptive. This applies generally, but particularly during, their menstrual period and the metabolic disarrangement of pregnancy. During this time some commonly acceptable smells are sufficiently repulsive to make them ill. It is not uncommon for women attending an education program spread over four weeks to report being more odour perceptive during their regular period.

Before commencing any sniffing, swirl the glass so that wine covers the whole available surface area of the glass. If you are a sloppy swirler, tilt the glass so a tongue forms up to the rim and then roll the glass around, coating the inside surface area.

The more coated surface area, the greater the release of odorous compounds. Another useful method of coating the total surface of the glass, and also exciting the wine, is to place your hand or a plastiglas lid over the top of the glass and shake it rather vigorously, then put it to your nose and start smelling before removing the cover. This is the second most important method for critical examination. See pages 67 and 68 for more details about methods of smelling.

Smelling and breathing are two separate functions, somewhat similar to walking and running. During normal breathing only a small amount of air contacts the smell receptor region, so a quick, deep, even forceful, sniff is desirable. Don't repeat this too quickly (no sooner than 30 seconds) as our smell organ fatigues easily. (Some people even find a forceful sniff counter productive and, of course, you don't want to hyperventilate.)

At the risk of labouring the point, it is important that you actually sniff the odours right up into the receptor area so that a worthwhile registration is made. At this time you will find that concentration is considerably aided by closing your eyes. Don't hold the glass under your nose and look at it as so many people do—sniff, and concentrate on nothing else. Should your smell power diminish, try smelling a glass of water or a can of coffee. This will give your smell mechanism some relief.

Concentration

A large part of the brain's processing of sensory signals involves filtering and selection of stimuli and information, and particularly that relating to our own needs or environment. If we don't concentrate, we allow important information to be filtered out. After sniffing the wine, spend plenty of time thinking through your first impressions. Practice will tell that often only one sniff is necessary—more than two or three sniffs are completely useless.

For a disciplined approach to smelling, make up your own check list: is the wine 'clean' (no dirty smells), fruity, sweet, varietal, woody, musty, oxidized, etc.? Record the good or bad features of aroma, bouquet and touch on a score sheet or 'spider' as illustrated later in the chapter (page 73). Working hand-in-hand with your score sheet (WER), particularly the right-hand column and the aroma wheel, here's a quick check list as a basis for your olfactory appraisal:

Check your results on the aroma wheel, working from the first tier, inside:

Aroma (from grape)	Irritation	Bouquet (from winery)
Fruity	No response	Clean
Floral	Sulphur—perceivable with irritation	Fresh
Spicy	Alcohol, irritating	Dirty
Vegetative	Perceivable sulphur - without irritation	Yeasty

Check list

Now have a look at the *intensity* **of smell.**

Negative (too little)	Positive	Negative (too much)
Latent —Dormant	Varietal	Out of balance i.e. too much wood or alcohol

fruity, vegetative, chemical, earthy—to the outside and more specific third tier: fruity, berry, strawberry, blackberry, raspberry, black currant.

The Nose

The 'nose' of the wine is made up from *aroma, bouquet* and *irritation*. Aroma is the fragrance provided by the fruit of the grape berry. Bouquet covers the winemaking process such as yeast, sulphurs, oak treatment, maturation and other good or bad smells not directly related to the fruit.

When commenting on the nose of a wine be careful in articulating aroma—the fruit; bouquet—the processing element, and irritation—the feel.

Repeated sniffing causes confusion, olfactory tiredness and contributes nothing to smell registration. So make sure that you complete your smelling and checking in an orderly fashion. Smelling requires practice, just as marathon running does, and it is an area in which, with practice, we can quickly lift our game.

Olfactory
tiredness

In the Brain

Let's stop at this point and consider what's going on at the central computer room—the brain, as the smell stimuli are fed into the system. A whole mass of signals are demanding answers. Signals from the olfactory centre and other signals of pain or irritation (the touch sense) in the nasal passage. It is at this time we can estimate the alcohol or SO_2 content of wine, as above average levels will cause physical irritation to the nose and, maybe, even the eyes.

Within a microsecond the brain is asked to provide answers to these smell and touch queries. You, and only you, can help at this time, a time demanding intense concentration and orderly analysis of all the signals. Use your score sheet (Wine Evaluation Record or WER) at this time, or some other recording sheet.

Smell Skills

Like a computer, the brain can only provide information that it has previously assimilated. In our case it must have a 'smell bank' if it is to interpret what we smell. To accumulate a smell bank it is good to become smell inquisitive and try to file away every identifiable odour. Herbs and spices in your kitchen are good training as many of these have the same fragrances as wine.

Exercise 2. During any spare moments, have a friend give you random tests with anything that will help you develop your smell skills. Also try to identify the smells in the glasses and cups in your cupboards. Practice makes perfect. If you use a towel for drying dishes it can be an amazing source of all types of kitchen odours, even the distinctive fragrances in the dishwashing detergent.

Smell
bank &
exercise

There are four defined areas of olfaction to be carefully considered. These are external, in-mouth, smell pathways and prior to in-mouth.

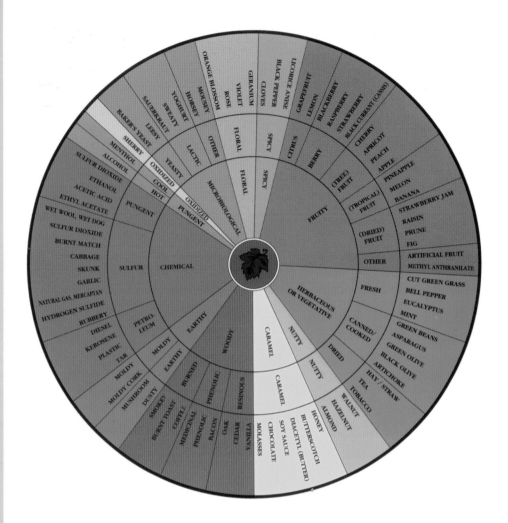

USING THE AROMA WHEEL

1. Select the general grouping from *tier 1*—such as *fruity.*

2. Move to *tier 2* and define the *fruity* group—such as *berry*

3. *Go to tier 3* and select the individual *berry* type—*blackberry.*

Describing wines in specific terms, such as those on the Wine Aroma Wheel, provides greater enjoyment and appreciation of the wonderful world of wine, plus an enhanced ability to discriminate and remember wine flavours.

Aroma Wheel by permission Dr. A C Noble UCD 2003.
To obtain copies contact Dr.Noble at:
acnoble@ucdavis.edu or www.winehardware.com

Method 1
Normal smelling

Method 2
Swirl and smell

Method 3
Retro-olfactory

Normal

Swirl

Shake

Hard palate

Soft palate

Air

Tongue

Wine

behind teeth

Whistle

backwards

Oesophagus

The recommended method is method 3: drop the chin against the chest, whistle backwards and suck air UP through the back of mouth (blue arrows).

DEFINED AREAS OF OLFACTION

External

The normally accepted method of smell appraisal is the straightforward smell up into the nose from the glass. It is my strong belief that this external effort is really only a 'warm-up' for the other more important smell appraisal methods.

In-Mouth

My main appraisal—the retro-olfactory—is made after the wine has been taken into the mouth (and then spat out, not consumed). This first gulp of wine is taken purely for olfactory, not taste or touch judgments. This retro-olfactory assessment is even more important if the wine is too cold for any worthwhile external judgement.

Nothing inhibits the natural fragrance of wine more than over-chilling—a common fault. With very few exceptions, all professional judgments of wine are made at room temperature; this is a tough time for professional tasters of champagne (and not a very pleasant experience).

Having taken a gulp, the best way to maximize your efforts here is to close your mouth, roll the wine around, chew it like a steak. This chewing action also brings into play other sensory receptors particularly in relation to texture.

Then drop your chin moving the wine into the area behind the bottom teeth. With pursed lips, suck in some air over the wine just as though you were eating hot soup. (Whistle backwards.) The wine, warmed by the saliva, will release more molecules of volatile substances. These will rise through the rear nasal passage to the smell receptors. The more molecules released, the more positive the registration. This is shown on page 67.

After the wine has been swallowed (spat-out for preference), close your mouth and breath out through your nose—or huff. This allows you to savour the wine. We smell by inhaling, savour by exhaling through the nose. This exhaling through the nose will also be a good indicator of which components are flavour and smell and which are taste. (Maybe, with very good wines, you can let a spoonful slip down your throat and this will certainly assist with critical flavour evaluations.)

Smell pathways—external and internal

Anyone who has ever smelt an empty beer or whisky glass the morning after a party will know that smells have a habit of hanging around, particularly bad smells. This is equally true of our empty wine glass that will have warmed somewhat following the disposal of the liquid, and have its total surface area coated, making available the maximum amount of smellable aroma.

Prior to In-Mouth Assessment

If we are alert and concentrating while the glass is being raised to the lips, almost immediately before the wine enters the mouth we will perceive the higher volatiles of the fruit flavour and bouquet. Watch very carefully for this bonus smell opportunity. It appears as though we unconsciously take a

Retro-olfactory

Smell hangs around

breath before placing things in our mouth and at this time we inhale some of the more prominent odours.

Regardless of the method of appraisal, it is worth remembering that too little wine will not allow for a worthwhile appraisal, while too much wine will prevent the mouth from warming it sufficiently to release an increased amount of volatile substances.

What Do We Actually Smell?

Here we run into three complexities

- Physiological   What can we really smell? *Do not be influenced by others.*
- Psychological   What do we anticipate or expect?
- Linguistic   Do we have the language resource to convey our sensory perceptions?

Too little- too much

In the first place we are smelling a coloured liquid and trying to relate this to some common everyday commodity so that we can communicate our experience. It is easy to say that a flower smells like rose when we can see or feel a rose, but we are looking at a glass of wine, not a rose. (By way of interest, Singaporeans are the only culture able to consistently identify rose fragrances—Caucasians are very poor at recognizing what one would think is an obvious smell.)

And what about the garlic-eating cultures of the world? Is this smell so ingrained that they can't smell two of wine's major faults— mercaptans and H_2S, both smelling somewhat similar to garlic. Certainly New Zealanders living near the famous Rotorua thermal fields are immune to the wine destroying odour of H_2S, a natural product of the local geysers.

What expectations does a French person have when smelling an Argentine wine—or a Moslem breaking the faith in favour of 'la dolca vita'? Can a top quality Catalonian or Australian product cross these formidable cultural barriers and be accepted in its own right?

Smell communication

Having determined what we think we can smell, it then becomes necessary to communicate our perceptions to others or there is no chance of elevating our appreciation of any art form. Verbalizing our sensory experiences is the short cut to greater pleasure. But that is easier said than done, without lots of practice.

Children have the benefit of their senses long before they are able to converse— just watch their reaction to good or bad offerings; and it's possible that the smell part of our brain predates useful conversation. Fetal infants have been observed in the uterus responding to tastes of sugar and other compounds. It has also been shown that if rat fetuses are exposed to the odour of ethanol while still in the uterus, they are more likely to be attracted to ethanol-flavoured water later in life.

Fetal infants

The stone age Fred Flintstone possibly lauded the merits of an underdone dinosaur rib fillet and jungle juice with the odd grunt. Many modern day wine lovers have the same tongue tied problem. *'I know what it smells/tastes like but can't explain it'* is an all too frequent response.

Wine lovers must start somewhere—here and now is a superb time and place to start correctly articulating our experiences. The fear of making a mistake is possibly the main cause of reticence for the novice taster, so let me hasten to assure you that even the most skilled professional is capable of, and makes, regular goofs.

As will be shown later, it is perfectly normal for perceptions to differ from one person to another. We, ourselves, are the only ones who are experts in our own perceptions—if we see red as red/brown and smell Chardonnay as grapefruit when others experience apricot, lime or melon, then these are our personal judgments. Where there is no absolute, I think your personal judgment is objective, not subjective as many people like to say. The very reason that there are so many wines on the market, and new styles appearing daily, is that winemakers and marketers wish to provide for all tastes. If there was one common taste there would be but one common wine.

Just to prove that you have nothing to fear about articulating your smell experiences, have a look at some of the more regular answers we receive to our tests with common fragrances:

> *Strawberry* has been called: Peach, cherry, vanilla, musk, cough medicine, apple juice, jelly beans, rose perfume, chewing gum, caramel, chocolate, mango, pineapple, apricot.
>
> *Ginger* has been called: Soap, three-in-one oil, turpentine, pine-gum, grass, gasoline, onion, rancid butter, lemon, citronella, moth balls, cedar, oil of cloves.
>
> *Apricot* has been called: Hard candy, mango, pineapple, Hawaiian punch, peppermint, strawberry, shampoo, orange, gingerbread.
>
> *Lychee* has been called: Musky, cedar, banana, caramel, strawberry, marzipan, toffee, coconut, fairy floss.

Conversely, there is not one fragrance in our repertoire of more than 50 common smells that has not, at sometime, been called strawberry.

Precision

Some years ago in New York, I was discussing the passionfruit character of a Riesling wine when, suddenly I was asked, 'What is passionfruit?'. Then I realized that this exotic fruit grew only in Australasia and Hawaii and unless wine lovers had visited that part of the world they could not relate to this smell. A similar or reverse situation occurred in New Zealand when people spoke about feijoa fragrances in wine—I hadn't previously experienced the smell or taste of this delicacy. (There is now a feijoa tree in our vineyard.)

So it's important when we are articulating our experiences that we use precise terms that can be understood. Such esoterics as 'cuddly', 'cheeky', 'delicate', 'elegant', 'pretentious', don't mean the same to everybody and therefore, are not precise terms and only confuse the people with whom you are trying to communicate. With this great confusion of words besieging us, it has been recognized for a long time that we should have a standard vocabulary for communicating wine perceptions.

Since this book was first published the corporate world and politicians have developed the art of double-talk. We now live in a world were it is difficult to understand what a lot of people say, even when they are speaking in the same language This is heightened by a group of under-educated wine communicators with a limited and personal vocabulary. Above all, as long as you use simple words and say exactly what you think, rarely will you be wrong—for you, anyhow.

Double talk

As mentioned in this chapter, we receive quite incredible results from smell tests during our seminars. For wine lovers wishing to identify (and you can) the smell differences between roses, new mown hay and violet, the first hurdle is to stop calling them room freshener—although this is one of their most common uses. When given the smell of ginger, some people write down bourbon. Why? Because they have ginger ale in their bourbon and ginger is the dominant odour of the mix. (Also, the ice in the drink usually dulls everything else.) These strange results are purely lack of training; remedies have been suggested earlier to help in this regard.

Strange results

Some years ago, it was my good fortune to present a series of seminars in California, Hawaii, New Zealand and Australia with Professor Ann C. Noble, a world authority in the smell field. In each new city, while on her daily jog, she would stop to smell any unusual flowers or shrubs. She is smell inquisitive, just as art lovers stop to look at paintings, or music lovers listen attentively to the sounds of music. I am assured that smell can be as sensuous and rewarding as any other art form.

My work around the globe indicates that the list below includes the necessary odours for the keen oenophile (and a must for anyone professionally engaged in the making, distribution or selling of wine) to be able to recognize. Be assured, it is impossible to have too much practice.

Professional involvment

I have presented both fresh blackberry juice and the synthetic blackberry flavour (as used in ice cream, cordial, milk shakes and pastries) in our seminars. Even though it is often identified as a 'berry' smell, a very small percentage of people recognize the blackberry flavour for what it is; not until recently, in South Africa, did several people identify blackberry juice, for the first time.

Cherry is another odour rarely recognised even though one regularly reads that this wine, or another, has 'overtones of cherry', or a 'cherry-like flavour'. So few people are able to recognize the smell of cherry, that one wonders if these critics know what blackberry or cherry really smell like?

ESSENTIAL ODOURS

Here is a list of chemical, fruit and floral odours to sharpen up your smell skills; of course, there are many more, but these are essential. If you have problems obtaining these odours, contact the International Wine Academy or Centre for International Wine Studies.

Chemical

Acetic acid	Vinegary.
Acetaldehyde	Distinctive smell of sherry.
Ethyl acetate	Nail polish remover, model aeroplane glue.
Diacetyl (dimethyl diketone)	Smell mixed into margarine to make it resemble butter. A by-product of malo-lactic fermentation that gives Chardonnay its 'buttery' smell. Also in beer, red wine, coffee, vinegar, and bay leaf oil.
Linalool	(individually) Floral, citric—and *Geraniol* (combined). Distinguishing odour of Riesling, Muscat and (Gewurz) Traminer wines.
Hydrogen sulphide	Rotten egg smell—rotten wine smell also.
Sulphur dioxide	The sulphur smell of a match when lit.
Ethyl alcohol	Ethanol, the main alcohol of wine.
Floral	Rose, violet, jasmine, geranium are but a few.
Fruity	Vine/berry fruit, tree fruits—tropical (mangos, bananas, papaya, lychee etc.), tree/stone fruits—other: citrus, pear, apple, fig, cherry, plum dried fruits (raisins, sultanas, prunes etc)—consider all of these as fresh canned, cooked, pureed; all as per the Aroma Wheel.
Spice	All spice, cinnamon, cloves, pepper.
Herbs	Mint, parsley—includes
Vegetable	Asparagus, bell pepper (capsicum), black & green olives, cabbage, garlic, onion, mushroom.

Words that smell

Acetaldehyde	The essential character of sherry, formed by oxidized alcohol.
Acuity	Keenness, sharpness.
Alcohol	A flammable, volatile, colourless liquid produced by the fermentation of sugars. Also called ethyl alcohol and ethanol. A major contributor to smell.
Aldehyde	Oxidation of primary alcohols. Important contributor to smell.
Aroma	The fragrance provided by the grape berry.
Bouquet	The part of the 'nose' made up from the winemaking and ageing processes. When combined with 'aroma' becomes the 'nose' of the wine.
Cilia	Smell receptors located in the olfactory epithelium.
Esters	Organic compounds formed by the union of an acid and an alcohol. With alcohol and aldehydes, they form the principal components of smell.
Fragrance	A sweet or pleasant odour.
Hydrogen Sulphide	Colourless gas formed by decaying vegetable matter. Commonly referred to as H_2S and identified as a rotten egg smell.
Mercaptans	A sulphur-containing organic compound, commonly used to give the smell in natural gas. Has a skunky or garlic smell.
Nose	The smell of wine that combines the bouquet, aroma and irritation.
Peptides	Natural or synthetic compounds containing at least two amino acids. Naturally occurring pituitary hormones.
Retro-olfactory	Retro-nasal. Smelling through the mouth.

WINE DETAILS		SIGHT 4 max	AROMA/ BOUQUET 6 max	IN MOUTH 6 max	AFTER FLAVOUR 2 max	OVERALL 2 max	TOTAL 20 max
1	Vintage *'04 Cullen* Variety *Chardonnay* Region *Margaret River*	4	5.25				
	Comments *Light gold colour–brilliant appearance, barrel-fermented, big on aromas of stone fruits and a little citrus.*						
2	Vintage *'04 Bouchard Pere* Variety *Chardonnay* Region *Le Montrachet*	3.5	4.75				
	Comments *Light straw colour–bright appearance, some melon & fig aromas, no apparent oak.*						
3	Vintage *04 Robert Mondavi* Variety *Chardonnay* Region *Napa CA*	3.75	5				
	Comments *Golden colour–appearance star bright, a wine with good promise, complex tropical fruits on nose—oak well balanced.*						
4	Vintage *'04 Hamilton Russell* Variety *Chardonnay* Region *Walker Bay, S.Africa*	4	5.25				
	Comments *Medium straw colour–brilliant appearance; bold style with some pear, tropical fruit & mineral aromas.*						
5	Vintage *'04 Floating Mtn* Variety *Chardonnay* Region *Waipara NZ*	4	5.50				
	Comments *Light golden colour–appearance star bright. Definitive citrus-pear- green apple, cold-climate aromas.*						

Wine evaluation record (WER) complete with SIGHT and Aroma/Bouquet scores and comments

Aroma and Bouquet

6 points	Extraordinary	Unmistakable characteristic aroma of grape variety. Outstanding and complex bouquet. Exceptional balance of aroma and bouquet.
5 points	Excellent	Characteristic aroma. Complex bouquet. Well balanced
4 points	Good	Characteristic aroma. Distinguishable bouquet.
3 points	Pleasant	Slight aroma and bouquet, but pleasant.
2 points	Acceptable	No perceptible aroma or bouquet.
1 point	Poor	Rating 3 above with slight off odours.
0 points	Objectionable	Objectionable and offensive off odours.

(Use decimal points or fractions where necessary)

Your scoring guide

AN IMPORTANT CHEMICAL CHAIN

Spend a few minutes to understand this relatively simple explanation of the main chemical components that the wine aficianado is normally confronted with. It will help to explain what is happening in your glass of wine.

1. Potassium bitartrate
2. Potassium metabisulphide(PMS) Tartaric acid exchange ions of H + for potassium to form the salt potassium bitartrate, the addition of (2) PMS to wine converts (2) to (1) potassium bitartrate and free SO_2.
3. Acetaldehyde is necessary to produce (4) ethanol + (7) CO_2 as it is the last stage of sugar conversion from (8) glucose into (4) and (7)
4. Ethanol. As (4) ethanol oxidizes—it becomes (3) acetaldehyde, which has a bonding affinity with (6) SO_2.
5. Tartaric Acid
6. SO_2 (Sulphur Dioxide)
7. CO_2 (Carbon Dioxide)
8. Glucose
9. Acetobactor. To produce (11) acetic acid (9) acetobactor must have O_2 to convert (4) ethanol into (3) acetaldehyde which it metabolizes to produce (11) and its ester (10) ethyl acetate. It is (10) that is volatile and that is what you smell.
10. Ethyl Acetate
11. Acetic Acid
12. O_2 (Oxygen)

SMELL SUMMARY

- Smell is the most important sense in the appraisal of food and beverages. Never forget this cardinal rule: be patient, don't rush past the smell appraisal.
- The most abundant volatiles are alcohols, aldehydes and esters. Only volatile substances are odourous.
- Most individuals perceive and respond differently to the same odour; very few odours can be considered absolute.
- Only a small percentage, about two per cent, of available odour finds its way to the smell receptors. Make the most of it.
- Each individual has a different level of smell acuity just as we each have smell 'blind spots'.
- Normal breathing brings only a minute amount of odour in touch with the smell organs. Make a positive sniff, upwards.
- Only one sniff is necessary, more than three are confusing.
- Close the eyes while smelling to help concentration.
- When the smell mechanism become fatigued, smell a glass of water.
- Our perceptions of smell differ from one individual to another and we each have a different level of acuity.
- Practice, practice, practice on the 'Odours to Learn' chemicals, fruits, flowers, herbs, spices and vegetables.
- Use words and language that are easily understood and portable from one group or place to another, even if it's on the other side of the world.

ELECTRONIC NOSES AND TONGUES

The new buzz words that wine lovers will be using in the near future are artificial neural networks—or ANN. Scientists the world over are working on this system that parallels the workings of our human nervous system and brain.

A five-minute surf through the web will tell you that most advanced countries are busy working in this area.

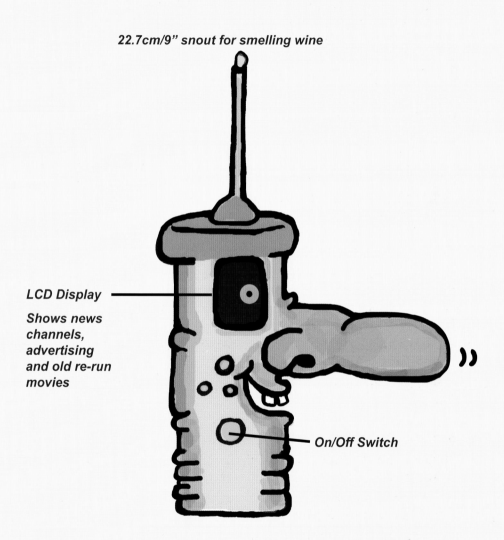

22.7cm/9" snout for smelling wine

LCD Display

Shows news channels, advertising and old re-run movies

On/Off Switch

Mark IV electronic nose with back-up human nose

In general, because of their development from the biological brain, ANNs are well suited to problems that people are good at solving—but not computers. However, unlike the human capability in pattern recognition, the ANN's capability is not affected by factors such as fatigue, working conditions, funerals, emotional state or today's football or tennis match.

Perfect or absolute

The down side, of course, is that these machines will be perfect or absolute, something that humans, in this field, are not. As mentioned several times elsewhere in the book, every person has his own, good or bad, threshold and perception for odours and tastants.

Electronic or artificial noses (E-noses) are being developed as systems for the automated detection and classification of odours, vapours, and gases. An electronic nose is generally composed of a chemical sensing system and a pattern recognition system.

This ability currently does many functions in the food, soft drinks and brewing industries such as detection of undesirable odours or excessive doses of various chemicals.

The chemical sensors are highly sensitive detectors whose conductance changes when volatile compounds come in contact with the intricate surface of the sensor and reacts with its sensitive materials. Just like babies, ANNs learn by example.

Industry problems

A current wine industry problem is the detection of sulphites and mercaptans in wine. Everybody has a different smell threshold for these faults in wine; many folks have a high threshold and are unable to smell low, but faulty, levels of these compounds. An E-nose does not have this problem, nor is it subjective.

The electronic tongue (E-tongue) measures dissolved organic and inorganic components i.e. non-volatile molecules that remain in the food or beverage.

Typically, E-tongues measure attributes like saltiness, sourness, bitterness and metallic tastes. Unless wine has been passed through an ion exchange column, saltiness has little application to the wine lover, but much to the food aficionado

Often I have used the expression that some wines are "like licking the side of a battleship". It will be marvellous to be able to measure the metallic and salt content of wine and learn if they actually did come from a vessel of war.

Speed and accuracy are the great advantages of these complimentary E-tongue and E-nose machines. A caffeine test done on the standard HPLC machine takes about 15 minutes while an E-machine will accurately complete the task in three minutes.

Here to stay

Fifteen years ago I thought that digital video was a myth, today it is a yawn in that it is the main standard in the video world. Electronic noses and tongues are here to stay and my prediction is that they will take over the quality control and other aspects of wine production, fermentation in particular, very shortly.

Yet I dread the thought of wines made solely by machines; then wine would become the same as cola or beer—and that is the worst nightmare that anyone could have!

SMELL MADE EASY

1. With few exceptions the major portion of wine and grape aromas come from the internal cells of the berry skin. In only a few varieties does the juice aroma dominate. I'm always fascinated when people talk about the 'typical' Cabernet or Chardonnay aroma. There is no such thing as typical, not even within one appellation.

   Even in Bordeaux, France, where Cabernet is nearly king, it is well documented that the Cabernet aromas vary considerably from one vineyard to another and this is without the influence of new oak. Their further different identification becomes a matter of psychology of smell, cultural background and the resource of language we have to describe it.

2. For aromas to reach the smell receptors they must pass through 18mm (or 3/4") of mucous membrane. Researchers believe that only 20 per cent of any available odour actually enters the nose, and of this amount only two per cent passes through the mucous membrane to make contact with the sensitive receptors.

3. Unless we concentrate and make maximum use of this limited smell resource, our natural gift of smell sensitivity and power will be wasted. Those who train and apply this wonderful sense will find new pleasures and skills, not only in food and beverages but also in many facets of their everyday life.

4. While we are smelling wine or food we can actually perceive physical irritation from, amongst other substances, alcohol and SO_2 through the free nerve endings in our nasal cavity.

5. Both alcohol and SO_2 are also 'touch' perceivable in the oral cavity; more about that in the next chapter. In the nasal cavity alcohol tends to irritate the bottom portion of the nose, whereas sulphur penetrates further-up to irritate and dry the upper portion of the nose. SO_2 is strongly reminiscent of a safety match being lit.

   Asthma sufferers should acquaint themselves with the smell of SO_2 which is widely used as a food preservative; and, wherever possible, avoid food or beverages containing SO_2.

6. During the olfactory assessment the most important part of the tactile sense is *temperature*. Even though it is comprehensively covered in a later chapter, it would be impossible to overstress its importance here. Wine that is too cold will have a 'dumb' nose—or no nose at all. Red wines that are normally served too warm, at room temperature, show far too much of the unpleasant alcohol content.

7. Before commencing any sniffing, swirl the glass so that wine covers the glass rght up to the rim. If you are unable to swirl without giving your friends a bath, then roll the glass around, coating the inside surface area so that a tongue forms up to the rim. At the risk of labouring the point, it is important that you consciously sniff the odours right up into the smell receptor area of the brain so that a worthwhile registration is made.

At this time you will find that concentration is considerably aided by closing your eyes. Don't hold the glass under your nose and look at it as so many people do—sniff, and concentrate on nothing else. Should your smell power diminish, try smelling a glass of water or a can of coffee. This will give your smell mechanism some relief

8. Practice will tell that, often, only one sniff is necessary—more than two or three sniffs are completely useless. Repeated sniffing causes confusion, olfactory tiredness and contributes nothing to smell registration. So make sure that you complete your smelling and checking in an orderly fashion. Smelling requires practice, just as marathon running does, and it is an area in which we can quickly lift our game with practice.

Within a micro-second, the brain is asked to provide answers to literally thousands of these smell and touch queries. You, and only you, can help at this time, a time demanding intense concentration and orderly analysis of all the signals. Be sure to use your score sheet (WER) to guide you in your determinations.

9. The 'nose' of the wine is made up from *aroma, bouquet* and (don't forget), *irritation.* Aroma is the fragrance provided by the fruit of the grape berry. Bouquet covers the winemaking process such as yeast, sulphur, oak treatment, maturation and other good or bad smells not directly related to the fruit.

10. When commenting on the nose of wine be careful in articulating aroma—the fruit (aroma); bouquet—the processing element, and irritation—the feel.

Note: USA regulations demand that all wines have warning labels (Contains Sulphites) if their sulphite levels exceed 10 parts per million.

SMELL—WORDS ABOUT FAULTS

BRETTANOMYCES
Bandaid
Barnyard*
Dekkera
Creosote
Dirty socks
Fishy
Fresh wool
Horsey
Leather & wet leather
Medicinal
Mousy
Phenolic
Smoky—BBQ
Strong spice
Wet animal

CORK TAINT
Musty
Mouldy
Water bag
Wet hessian-
USA gunny-
sack

OXIDISED
Aldehydic
Bad apple
Dank—as in old-cellar
Mouldy
Musty
Nutty
Sherry-like
Wet bags-hessian
Wet paper

SULPHIDES
Boiled potatoes
Burnt rubber
Cabbage
Garlic
Onion
Rotten eggs
Skunky
Stagnant water

VOLATILE ACID
Acetic (acid)
Ethyl acetate
Model aero glue
Nail polish remover
Vinegar (wine)

OTHER
Bacon-fat
Baked
Cooked
Geranium
Microbial
Stemmy
Weedy

These are all faults that occur in the winemaking process. The important issue here is how differently people verbalise the same odour. Listed are 16 only descriptors for brettanomyces (brett), yet there are many, many more in peoples' vocabulary.

*Barnyard is a common North American descriptor that groups together many things e.g. all sorts of animal smells and manures, rotting leaves and vegetation etc; use it cautiously.

WHITE WINE VARIETAL AROMAS

CHARDONNAY
Almonds
Apples
Apricots
Banana
Celery
Citrus—lemon/lime
Cucumber
Fig
Nectarines
Nuts— hazelnut
           walnuts
Peaches—fresh & canned
Pears
Pineapple—fresh/canned
Tropical fruit salad

PINOT GRIS
Apple
Apricot
Citrus
Floral
Grapefruit
Guava
Honey
Lavender
Lychee
Mango
Musk
Nectarine
Passionfruit
Pear
Perfumed
Rose
Spices
Tropical fruit
Violet
White peach

RIESLING
Apple—Granny
 Smith
Citrus—lemon
  "   lime
  "   blossom
  "   orange peel
Floral
Grapefruit
Guava
Honeysuckle
Jasmine
Kerosene
Fly spray
Melons
Mineral
Musk
Passionfruit
Pear
Perfumed
Pineapple
Quince
Rose
Spices
Mixed tropical fruit

SEMILLON
Apple—green
Citrus
Cut grass
Fig
Green bean
Hay
Honey
Lemon
Pear
Peas
Quince,
Topical fruit salad

CHENIN
Hay
Herbal
Honey
Lemon
Peach
Pear
Quince
Tropical fruit

Traminer

SAUVIGNON
Apple—Granny
 Smith
Celery
Citrus
Dill
Flint
Freshly cut grass
Gooseberry
Grapefruit
Green peas
Mango
Melon
Mineral
Passionfruit
Tropical fruit
Vegetal

TRAMINER (Gewurz)
Floral
Grapefruit
Green apple
Hazelnut
Honey
Lime
Lychee
Mango
Marmalade
Melon
Nectarine
Peach
Perfumed
Pineapple—fresh
Quince
White peach

VIOGNIER
Apricot
Artichoke
Asparagus
Citrus—orange blossom
  "   orange peel
Floral
Green bean
Honey
Marmalade
Melons
Peach
Pear
Perfumed
Tomato leaf
Tropical fruit

Sauvignon

RED WINE VARIETAL AROMAS

CAB. SAUVIGNON
Beans—green
Bell pepper/capsicum
Berry—blackberry
"   raspberry
"   strawberry
Cassis—black currant
Cigar box
Eucalyptus
Herbaceous
Leather
Mint
Olives
Pepper—black
Soy—in older wines
Stone fruit—cherry
"   plum
"   prune
Tea
Tobacco
Vegetative—asparagus
             cabbage
             B.sprouts

GRENACHE
Dominated by intense:
Berry flavours
Cherry
Olives—and many of
the Syrah aromas

NEBBIOLO
Black plum
Camphor
Coffee
Cherry
Scented
Stone fruit—cherry
"   plum
Tar
Truffles
Violets

MERLOT
Berry fruit—blackberry
Caramel
Cassis—black currants
Cherry
Cocoa
Jammy
Licorice
Plums
Smoky
Tobacco
Toffee—and many
of the Cabernet
aromas

TEMPRANILLO
Earthy
Herbaceous
Spice
Stone fruit—cherry
"   plum
Tobacco

PINOT NOIR
Animal
Berry— black
          raspberry
          strawberry
Cassis
Cinnamon
Floral—violet
Mint
Sous bois—French
for rotting-leaves
Stone fruit—cherry
"   plum
Perfumed

PINOTAGE
Almond
Raspberry
Earthy
Mineral
Varnish

SYRAH
Berry:—black
"   mulberry
"   strawberry
Dried fruit—raisins
Gamey
Grilled meat
Hickory
Melted caramel
Pepper—black
Saddle-leather
Smoked bacon
Soy
Spicy
Stone fruit—
          cherry
          plums
Tar
Tobacco
Truffles
Violets

ZINFANDEL
Artificial fruit
Confectionery
Mixed berry
Pepper
Plum
Raisin
Soy
Spicy

SANGIOVESE
Cherry
Earthy
Leather
Savoury
Strawberry

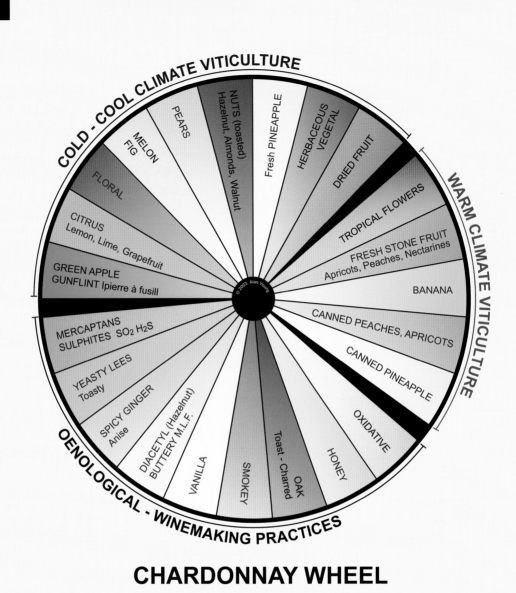

CHARDONNAY WHEEL

Aroma and bouquet source descriptors.

1. In normal years, cold-cool climate viticulture provides fruit with more acid. More particularly, fruit of the citrus range lemon, lime, grapefruit—also fresh pear, fresh pineapple with lots of acid.

2. Warm climate viticulture normally provides fresh stone fruit flavours such as apricots, peaches and nectarines. You will also find pineapple but more like the canned fruit with ample sweetness.

3. Chardonnay, more than most other wines, can be sculptured and shaped during the winemaking process. This provides the buttery, lactic, butterscotch hazelnut flavours

CHAPTER 5

No matter how much we learn about the brain we can never learn it all. There will always be something to astound us, to amaze us, to keep us humble, while at the same time stimulating us to greater efforts toward understanding the brain. The human brain is simply the most marvellous organ in the known universe.

—Dr. Miles Herkentham, National Institute of Mental Health, USA (1992)

From the brain and the brain only arise our pleasures, joys, laughter and jests as well as our sorrows, pains, griefs and fears.

—Hippocrates (400BC)

THE HUMAN BRAIN

The brain is the source of all our dreams, our moods, our thoughts, our actions. The brain is 1.36kg (or 3lbs) or more, of tens of billions of nerve cells (neurons) and many more billions of glial (supporting) cells. Its ceaseless day and night activity needs massive amounts of oxygen and calories, derived mainly from glucose. These, as well as other necessities such as amino acids, ions and hormones, are transported or diffused across the protective blood-brain-barrier into the brain.

The complexity of the inter-connections of these billions of nerve cells and their ability to process information defies the imagination. It is estimated that some of them may have ten thousand or more connections with other neurons. Brain input from smell and taste (the chemical senses) receptors are now known to affect not only olfaction (smell) and gustation (taste) but also behavior, memory and learning, various emotional states and possibly other activities essential to both mental and physical well-being.

Defies imagination

Neural Communication

The largest number of neurons is found in the central nervous system—the spinal cord and the brain. The peripheral nervous system, including its autonomic (a number of the body's self-governing systems) components, extends a network of nerve fibres over the entire body.

Neurons communicate with each other by a combination of electrical and chemical signals in a complicated series of events. The message is usually carried *electrically within* each neuron, and *chemically between* neurons. The events start with an induced change of membrane potential causing a flow of sodium ions through the membrane followed, within a few hundred microseconds, by a reverse flow of potassium ions (an electrically charged atom) to the outside of the membrane. The nerve impulses thus generated, travel down the length of the axon to the nerve terminal. There, a change in the electrical conductance of the terminal membrane admits calcium into the terminal.

Chemically & electrically

This 'firing' releases a chemical messenger, a neuro-transmitter, which diffuses across the tiny synaptic cleft (the point of contact between cells) that separates neurons. The transmitter, in turn, initiates changes in the ionic conductance of the postsynaptic membrane to produce either excitation or inhibition, in a sort of 'go' or 'no-go' manner. Actually the result is more complicated because the neuron has a mechanism for integrating the totality of the excitatory and inhibitory inputs and expressing that net sum by its own rate of discharge or 'firing'. It can do its own thing!

Human actions are ultimately the net result of decisions made by the central nervous system resulting from many input channels. *The effect of inputs is presumed to differ from individual to individual.* In other words, whether we cut our finger, see a great painting, hear a superb orchestra or taste an excellent glass of wine—all sensations travel to the cerebral cortex for interpretation, judgment and decisions; the reactions occur in the finger, the eye, the ear

Go—no go

or the mouth, but only after orders (the motor signals) from the brain have returned to the point of contact.

When we cut a finger, a message flashes to the brain, the sense of pain speeds to the finger and another complex mechanism files away a message telling you to be more careful next time you use a sharp knife. Some people make a major performance of a cut finger, others ignore the same problem.

THE CHEMICAL SENSES

Olfaction (Smell)

Our knowledge of the mechanism of olfaction is far from complete. Some of the most important odour information processing takes place within the mucous layer of the olfactory epithelium at the top of the nasal cavity. Odour molecules link to specialized receptor sites (lock and key molecules-see Olfactory Chapter) on the membranes of the hairline cilia attached to the millions of olfactory neurons found there.

Not yet known

It is not yet known whether there are specific receptors for specific odours, but we do know that olfactory receptors can monitor the environment with great precision. Humans, as well as many other animals, can distinguish odour resulting from quite small variations in the chemical structures of the odour molecule.

The central parts of the olfactory nerves enter the two olfactory bulbs which are immediately behind the nose, one on either side of the middle of the brain. The anatomy and chemistry of the bulbs are distinctive and in several ways unlike most other brain regions.

Chemical substances which modify or block the action of neurotransmitters found in the bulbs should have major effects upon the olfactory process. For example, since the bulbs are rich in opiate binding sites, substances which alter binding to these sites could conceivably alter olfactory perception. The application of new molecular tools to the study of olfactory receptors may also answer fundamental questions about odour recognition and permit the development of agents with highly selective effects.

Sexual behaviour

Neural signals pass from the olfactory bulbs to other parts of the limbic system and then to the cerebral neo-cortex. It is through these further connections that the olfactory systems affect overall brain functioning including learning and memory, sexual behavior and regulation. The neurotransmitters which are most highly concentrated in the limbic system include many that are known to mediate actions of the major agents that relieve the symptoms of mental illness. The principal anti-schizophrenic, anti-depressant and anti-anxiety drugs are thought to owe their therapeutic effects to their influence upon the limbic system.

Scientists usually solve complicated problems by investigating relatively simple systems that can be models for complex ones. The olfactory system may provide a relatively simple model for more study of the general brain.

A. **thalamus** part of the brain stem; a mass of nerve cells that organises and relays sensory information

B. **pons** a short section of the brain stem that serves as a communication bridge between the cerebrum and the cerebellum

C. **medulla oblongata** the part of the brain stem that links the pons and the spinal cord; controls body functions such as respiration and circulation

D. **nasal cavity** the passageway between the external nasal openings and the pharynx; filters, warms, and moistens incoming air

Valuable information

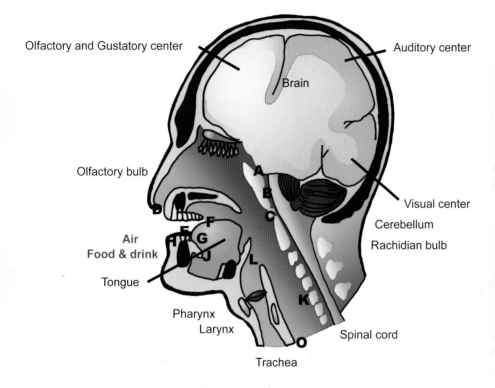

Olfactory and Gustatory center

Auditory center

Brain

Olfactory bulb

Visual center

Cerebellum

Rachidian bulb

Air
Food & drink

Tongue

Pharynx
Larynx

Spinal cord

Trachea

Where it all happens

E. **maxilla** and mandible upper and lower jawbones

F. **upper palate** the roof of the oral cavity; the bony part in front is the **hard palate**, the soft tissue portion in the back is the **soft palate**

G. **oral cavity** the cavity bounded by the lips, cheeks, tongue, and palate

H. **teeth** the incisors; chisel-shaped teeth for cutting

J. **tongue** a muscular organ used in chewing, swallowing, and speaking

K. **spinal cord** main pathway of the nervous system; transmits incoming sensory informaticri and outgoing motor impulses

L. **pharanx**—the throat; the passageway to the trachea and oesophagus

M. **epiglottis** a flap of cartilage that closes over the trachea (windpipe) to prevent food or fluid from entering

N. **oesophagus** the tube through which food passes to the stomach

CHAPTER 6

Only if you are an identical twin from the same egg can you expect to have the same sense of taste. Each of you has your own sense of taste, own sense of smell.

—Dr. Morley R. Kare
Founder and former director,
Monell Chemical Senses Center

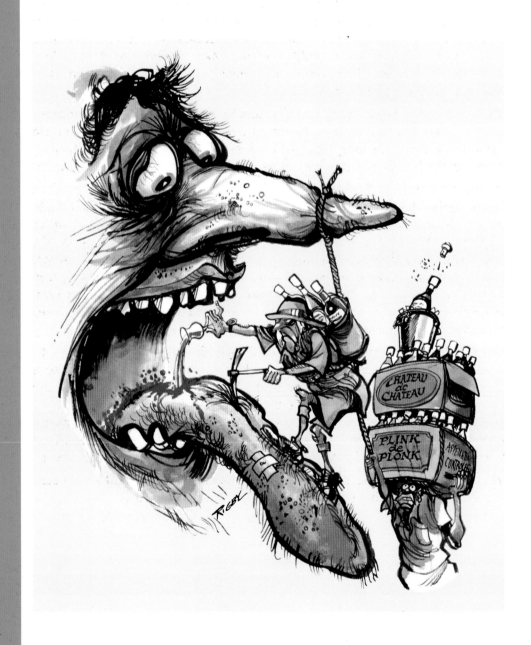

TASTE—GUSTATION

Our knowledge of the mechanism of *gustation* is greater than that of *olfaction*, but it is still incomplete. The common perception of flavour is actually a combination of odour and taste inputs plus texture and temperature. Here we are concerned only with the five basic tastes bitter, salt, sour, sugar and umami.

Taste and smell interact closely in determining our appreciation of food and wine. Early man utilized the sense of taste to monitor poisons, which were often bitter, from calorically valuable foods which tended to be sweet. Taste is important for modern man as well. Many diseases, medications and other therapies interfere with our ability to taste. Many of those so affected lose any interest in eating. Frequently they develop psychiatric disturbances in addition to physical deterioration.

Taste perception begins with specific receptor cells in the taste buds located primarily on the tongue but also on other parts of the oral cavity. While numerous, the taste receptors are far less in number than the olfactory receptors. Unlike the olfactory receptors, the taste receptors are not themselves neurons but connect with neurons whose processes lead to the brain.

Small variations in chemical structure can cause major alterations in taste as well as in smell. Very minor variations in the amino acid structure of peptides can transform a molecule totally from sweet to bitter. Presumably, specific receptor sites exist on the membranes of the taste cells which interact selectively with flavour molecules. And as with the olfactory system, it is likely that applying the new, powerful molecular tools of neuroscience may make it possible to isolate these taste receptors and work out the mechanism whereby we recognize and discriminate between flavours.

The taste cells communicate with neural taste fibres which in turn travel to a relay station in the brainstem, the nucleus of the solitary tract, and from there to the pons (a communication bridge), the thalamus and ultimately the cortex. The solitary tract influences much of the body's internal environment such as blood pressure regulation and vomiting. This is almost certainly why extremely bad tasting food makes us nauseous presumably to protect us from poisons. Similarly, a fall in blood pressure can make us feel faint and nauseous.

There is so much to learn, even though Hippocrates had it right 2,500 years ago—little wonder that he is the 'father' of modern medicine.

TASTE

Precise words are one of the main factors in wine evaluation—so let us start by carefully defining 'taste'. As the word, technically, applies only to the five basic tastes of sugar, sour, salt, bitter and umami, we should really use the words *evaluation, judging* or *assessment* in place of the misused and misleading generalized word *tasting*. If all one is purely tasting (putting the wine in the mouth and swallowing) the wine, then use the word tasting but if you are judging the wine for any reason, use a worthy word.

After all, this is a book about sensory evaluation.

The Palate

Wine writers comments

If any one word in the English language is used, misused, over-used and abused it is the word *palate*. One thing is for sure; anyone who uses this word in relation to wine judgement is either living in the 19th century or does not understand what they are saying. Have a look at this from one writer: 1. 'These also dominate the young palate, developing into an unctuous long-lasting palate showing ginger and spices…' 2. 'The youthful palate of The Hermit Crab is…' 3. 'The palate is filled with herbaceous fruit…; while from another writer, 'The palate was so strong it went right through the nose.' These are comments about wine; if you understand this frivolity, you are way ahead of me. The word *palate* raises two pertinent questions. What is the palate—and where is it?

Two palates

Firstly, we have two palates—the soft and hard palates. Secondly, the soft palate at the rear of the mouth does perceive taste; most scientists say that the hard palate, or the roof of the mouth, has no taste receptors in which case how can it have anything to do with the sense of taste?

It is impossible to over-state how differently each of us perceives the same stimulus and the strength with which we perceive that stimulus. Every person alive has a different threshold for each of the senses. In other words we are not all the same as many wine experts would have us believe.

Instead of palate, why not use the word *mouth*; isn't this where the wine or food is? As you go through the various taste and touch exercises, you will learn that each person perceives these components in a different place in the mouth—and at a different strength and threshold.

The threshold is the intensity below which a stimulus cannot be perceived and cannot produce a response. Each of us is very different in our threshold for all taste, touch and smell sensations, as you will learn when you work with this book—and with your friends.

Analyse methodically

On pages 193–4 you will see a format for telling the world, or your friends, exactly what you thought about a particular wine. This is a disciplined approach so that you cover every facet of what you experienced. You can only do this if you methodically analyse each of the components – and not lump them all together with the one-size-fits-all word—palate.

Taste is a very limited sense due to the physiological makeup of the taste receptors. When we eat food or drink wine the various nerves, from three different senses in our mouth, come into play and provide us with an *overall flavour impression*.

Many people think that when we have a cold we lose our sense of taste. This is not correct. We lose our sense of smell; taste is rarely affected. An apple, potato and onion all smell quite different, but a blindfolded person, deprived of smell, would be hard-put to differentiate the taste of these three similarly textured products. Try it next time you have a cold. If, by necessity, we were tube fed a superb three-course meal from our favorite restaurant, our hungry tummies would taste and smell nothing.

Taste exercise #1 This is really a three senses exercise: taste, touch and smell. Place a peg on your nose and a blindfold over your eyes (no cheating), have a friend serve you a spoon of chopped apple and another serve of chopped onions and see if you can tell the difference. You can do the same thing with a handful of mixed jelly beans; use a peg on your nose, close your eyes and select any of the jelly beans in your hand. As long as you play the game fairly, you will receive an enormous shock about flavour.

A big shock

So it is of prime concern to the budding sensory evaluator/judge that taste is recognized for what it is—a very limited sense; and our efforts should be concentrated in the discrimination of the overall flavour impressions—taste, smell and the two touch components: temperature and texture.

Overall flavour

It is a tragedy that so many influential critics know so little about the inter-relationship of all the physical senses involved in enjoying wine, and talk indiscriminately about 'taste'. Even worse, many dictate that there is, or should be, a 'common' taste for each product from wine down to even such a mundane commodity as bread. There isn't—and I daresay there never will be.

Front of Mouth

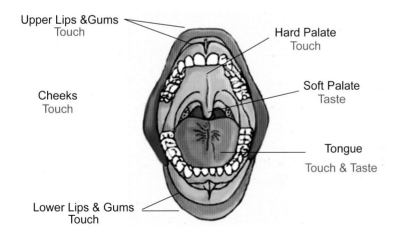

Upper Lips &Gums
Touch

Hard Palate
Touch

Cheeks
Touch

Soft Palate
Taste

Tongue
Touch & Taste

Lower Lips & Gums
Touch

Learn about Taste

It is thought that the taste insensitivity in humans is brought about because our taste receptors are unsophisticated by comparison with other animals, and, as individuals, we do ever so little to train any of our senses. For reasons unknown, we teach children about sight and colour, teach them the enjoyment of sound but not about smell or taste.

Unanswered questions

The lack of knowledge, the difficulty in measuring taste responses (even trained people can only give about 40 per cent accurate response) and the difference between animals used in laboratory tests and human subjects, makes for a lack of positive statements about the taste sense. Bearing that in mind, I'll keep saying 'possibly', 'we believe', 'it is understood' etc. because, in this 21st century, there are so many unanswered questions regarding the senses of taste, touch and smell.

Unlike the smell, sight and hearing receptors, which as primary sensory cells, combine the functions of transduction (receiving) and conduction (sending), the taste receptors are not neurons sending their own messages to the brain; they function only as receivers (transducers).

This simply means that the other sensory receptors pick up the signal, be it sight, hearing or smell, and the receptor sends that message. With taste, the receptor has to go through a switchboard and hook onto a neuron to send its message. We believe that taste receptors are continually mobile, degenerating and regenerating and are far fewer in number than the olfactory receptors.

In fact, *we don't taste flavour in our mouth*, we actually perceive the signals and then assemble them all together, make decisions such as 'I like' or 'I do not like' in the brain, and then these messages are relayed back to the mouth.

PHYSIOLOGY OF TASTE

Tongue's surface

The surfaces of the oral cavity, i.e. the tongue and the soft palate, (epiglottis and larynx, mainly in children) are covered with the epithelium layer which contains four types of papillae (Latin = nipple) which are the roughness (or velvet) of the tongue's surface. I believe they are also on the lips and cheeks. Three types contain taste chemo-receptors (taste buds) measuring about .07mm deep and .05mm wide, which are located in the depressions of the papillae. See page 118.

The filiform taste buds are mechano-receptors rather than chemo-receptors and register the touch sense only.

Taste buds house taste cells and taste pores. The actual sensation of taste is perceived by finger-like microvillia (see page 118) attached to the taste cells poking through the pores within the taste bud. Four types of taste buds, known as papillae, are located in the oral cavity:

• *Filiform* papillae—spread over the entire tongue. These are the most numerous but lack *taste* receptors. Their function is the tactile sense—or *touch*. While not being taste receptors, they have an even more important role in registering temperature (hot and cold), pain or irritation caused by high levels of alcohol or hot spices, bubbles, tannin and other items fully dealt with in the next chapter.

• *Fungiform* papillae—are mushroom-shaped *taste* buds that have receptors on the upper surfaces and are widely distributed

- *Circumvallate* papillae—are large circular flat papillae with the taste receptors in a moat-like channel. There is considerable debate about the location of circumvallate buds. Some say they are located on the sides of the tongue—others say in the V of the tongue. Most agree that they occupy the rear two thirds of the tongue.

- *Foliate* papillae—common in animals but minimally present in humans.

Taste buds contain 50–100 taste cells with finger-like microvilli protruding from each cell and these poke through the taste pore at the top of the taste bud. So, we have taste *buds*, taste *cells* and taste *pores* all working to respond to our eating and drinking.

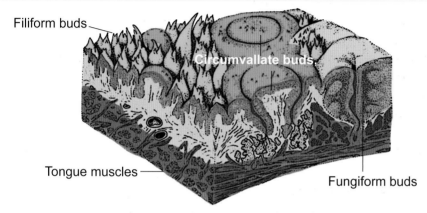

After experimenting with solutions made up from the suggested components, it is possible that you will find these generalizations really do vary with the individual. The fact that children lick sugar candy and ice cream with the tip of their tongue, whereas Dad heaves his beer to the rear of his mouth enabling the bitterness of the brew to be perceived, does not in any way support the general idea of special areas of taste sensitivity.

Unlike the receptors of sight and hearing, taste receptors are continually being replaced, some 3000–5000 daily, or a complete change at about weekly intervals. What were once thought to be different sizes and types of taste buds are known to be developing or degenerating receptors. On the positive side, this could be a clever built-in safety mechanism because if we burn our tongue the affected taste buds will be replaced within a week. The receptors of our other senses are thought to be irreplaceable. (It is now known that we also have a turnover of smell receptors.)

The negative side is that this regular movement possibly accounts for our lack of sensitivity in taste. Whereas the eye can make some 7,000,000 comparative judgments, the smell and hearing receptors are also super sensitive, we need a 30 per cent increase or decrease in a given substance before the *taste threshold* can register a difference. A classic example is acetic acid which tastes the same as most other wine acids, yet the smell threshold of ethyl acetate is something like 24 000 times lower than the taste threshold.

Five Basic Tastes

The common belief (but one no longer enjoying any scientific credence) is that we have four basic tastes that, although widespread in the oral cavity, are said by many people who should know better, to be conveniently grouped:

Pre-historic rubbish

- Sweet registering on the tip of the tongue.
- Salt impressing the taste buds on either side of, and over the top of, the tongue near the front.
- Sour also along the sides of the tongue, but further back.
- Bitter on the rear top of the tongue.

It is hard to believe that after the first publication of this book nearly 20 years ago, some universities still teach this outdated theory. Can you believe that this

Not all tongues have this distinctive V in the centre. Check yours in the mirror.

Fungiform papillae are widely distributed. Taste is perceived on the top surface of the tongue.

misconception stems from a faulty 1901 translation from the German language. Extensive international research now tells us that these taste sensations are widely spread over all portions of the tongue and other parts of the oral cavity.

More bad news

Forever bearing in mind that we are individuals, how our taste receptors work is essential to a correct understanding of what is happening in our mouth and brain.

Most of us are born with two legs which enable us to walk, run and jump, yet only a small fraction of one percent of the population ever achieve Olympic status in walking, running or jumping which requires enormous training effort. Similarly, we achieve our level of wine or food expertise conditional on our input and practise.

When born, we fall into one of three categories of tasting ability which have been given these strange titles relating to the number of taste buds per square centimetre according to their ability to detect n-PROP (n-propylthiouracil:

Non-tasters to supertasters

- A *non-taster* has 54 fungiform papillae/cm^2 (120 taste pores/cm^2)
- A taster has 73 fungiform papillae/cm^2 (350 taste pores/cm^2)
- A supertaster has 98 fungiform papillae/cm^2 (668 taste pores/cm^2)

This is all marvellous, if one has the knowledge and ability to train one's senses, which very few people have unless they go to a training institution and participate in an ongoing program, or read literature such as this. There is no short-cut in sensory appraisal.

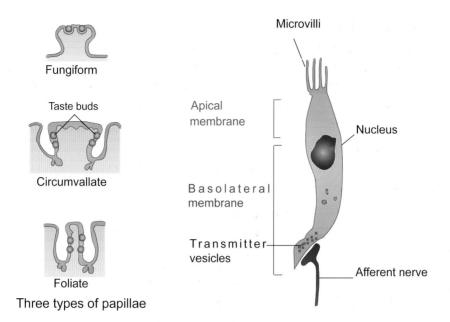

Fungiform

Taste buds

Circumvallate

Foliate

Three types of papillae

Microvilli

Apical membrane

Nucleus

Basolateral membrane

Transmitter vesicles

Afferent nerve

The mouth is host to the sensations of taste, smell and touch. When we eat or drink, what are known as tastants enter our mouth. These are the chemicals in the food or drink and they become associated with our saliva. These various chemicals instantly find their way onto the taste cells and through an amazing series of connections register in the brain.

Sapid Substances

The perception of sapid (those having taste) substances is somewhat similar to the lock and key principle discussed in the Olfaction Chapter. These sapid substances have both mineral and organic backgrounds. Electro-physiological (laboratory tests using electrical pulses) recordings of the potential from single taste cells show that they are sensitive to more than one basic substance, with different cells having different patterns of relative sensitivities.

The taste cells, apparently, code preferentially rather than individually. Although smell molecules have a habit of 'hanging around', taste molecules are easily washed away, with the exception of bitter compounds and the sweetener aspartame.

There is no question that each person's taste perception is as individual as is her or his pulse beat or fingerprints. Temperature plays a key role in these taste responses and is discussed at length in the following chapter on the tactile sense.

No question

The taste sense becomes active early in our life. Babies (even before birth) immediately respond to sugar, salt, lemon juice and quinine that stimulate the four of the accepted taste areas. Babies seem to like sweet tastes, maybe mother's milk shapes this affinity—but dislike the rest. By the time we reach adulthood most people grow to accept salty and sour tastes but, in terms of consumers, it is mainly the beer drinkers who acquire any taste for bitterness, even though a lot of coffee and red wine are considered to be bitter.

Such perception of bitterness could be a relative cultural idiosyncrasy. Most Americans who taste Vegemite® or Marmite® (two brand names) find these popular spreads far too salty. Yet most Australians would not consider it so; it is fed to babies on bread and butter. It's a general belief that some poisonous natural foods (berries, leaves and roots) are known to be bitter, whereas sweet things in the wild tend to be life sustaining.

Saliva

The mouth is almost continually lubricated through sets of glands that open into various parts of the cavity. These glands are known as parotid, sublingual and submandibular. Without saliva we would have no taste, only the sense of touch.

The taste receptors respond to substances dissolved in the oral fluids (saliva) bathing them, and the importance of the chemical composition of the saliva in our mouth has yet to be properly understood. One popular theory suggests that the sodium level of saliva varies quite markedly during the course of a day. Aside from psychological factors, this, I believe, accounts for similar glasses of wine having what appears to be a different taste in the morning and evening, or from one day to another.

It is pleasing to note that research work is continuing on the fascinating subject of the chemical makeup of the saliva. There is no doubt in my mind that this, more than anything else, accounts for the differences in our taste preferences. However, we do know that our taste threshold lowers considerably when we rinse our mouth with distilled water. We are then able to perceive basic tastes at lesser concentrations.

As mentioned above, we are all different in our perception and taste thresholds of wine components; it is recommended that you carefully record the impressions of the various components on your teeth, gums, cheeks and the rest of the oral cavity. With training, we are able to perceive three different threshold levels, over and above a blank sample of distilled water.

1. The minimum concentration is referred to as the *detection* threshold.
2. The next stage is the identification threshold where we can both *detect* and *identify* the substance.
3. Being able to *quantify* the substance is the difference threshold.

At all times be conscious of the difference between the five basic *tastes* and the *tactile* senses of hot/cold, rough/smooth, pain/irritation, oily.

COMPONENTS OF TASTE

Acids

Of all wine components, natural fruit acids, which make wine sour and different from other beverages, are the most important contributors to the life, balance and refinement of wine. Apart from their flavour benefits, acids also protect wine from spoilage. However, there are three groups of acids involved in wine, including mineral and organic. In food and beverages mineral acids are only in minute traces if at all, and are noted for their aggressiveness. These are sulphuric, nitric and hydrochloric acids. The organic acids are malic, tartaric, citric and lactic.

These can be further broken down into groups by origin. Acids that originate in the grape berry are the natural fruit acids—malic, tartaric and citric. Then there are the acids that originate during fermentation and through microbiological reaction during evolution or maturation—lactic, acetic, succinic, formic and propionic to name a few of the more important ones. These acids are important contributors to wine aroma.

There are also non-volatile and volatile acids. The natural fruit acids—malic, tartaric and citric are non-volatile, while those produced during fermentation such as lactic, acetic, succinic, formic and propionic are volatile.

Malic and tartaric are the main acids of wine while citric, lactic and others that are in limited quantities, assist with flavour and balance. Malic acid occurs in many fruits including grapes, apples and gooseberries. Tartaric is mainly a grape acid and is known to dominate in warm viticultural area fruit; malic acid seems to predominate in cooler areas. The longer, slower ripening conditions in cool climates apparently inhibits malic acid respiration from the berry.

It is unfortunate that acid is classified in the sour/salt taste groupings. While acid does certainly contribute to sourness, the terms acid and sour have totally different connotations in wine evaluation language. Crisp clean acidity gives wine life and lightness whereas sourness, as such, is very much a negative term.

When discussing acidity in wine, pH (p for power, H for hydrogen ion concentration) always rears its head. pH, as mentioned in the colour chapter, is all important in wine quality but is more applicable to winemaking than wine evaluation.

The pH Factor

pH is an expression of hydrogen ion concentration in solution. An ion is an atom that has an electrical charge and is not bound to another atom. The pH scale ranges from 1 to 14, pH 7 is neutral; pure distilled water is pH 7 or neutral. Below pH 7 a solution moves toward acidity, above pH 7 the solution is alkaline. (pH measurements are commonly used to determine garden soil acid/alkaline levels and this soil balance can have a strong influence on grape juice pH.) Above 3.8 wine has so little acid that it is flat, between 3.2 and 3.6 wine is microbiologically stable; lemon juice is about 2.3, and O is total acidity.

Winemakers look for figures between p H 3.00 and pH 4.00. The lower the pH figure the higher the acidity but winemakers are often frustrated by high pH and high acid levels in some viticultural areas, usually those with high potassium in the soil. A light style Riesling is more likely to be near pH 3.00 whereas a fuller bodied wine, i.e. Chardonnay or Sauvignon would be at the higher end.

Desirable pH levels in wine are:

- White table wines   pH 3.00–3.40
- Red table wines   pH 3.30–3.70+
- Dessert wines   pH 3.50–3.80

Relativity is the dominant factor about pH. Low pH factors will give light bodied wines such as the classic Rieslings of the Mosel, Rhine, Canada, southern Australia, New Zealand and New York State. But, this low figure is relative to the winegrowing region and the wine style. Take as an example Cabernet and Riesling wines from the cool regions of Chile and Rheingau (Germany) and compare them with those from the warm inland irrigated areas of California or Australia.

The Chilean and German wines must have figures of 3.3-3.5 and 3.0-3.2 respectively to retain their classic styles, whereas in the warmer regions a Cabernet at 3.5 pH and a Riesling at 3.4 would still be considered excellent wines. This is because warm area fruit attains a degree of ripeness beyond the capabilities of cool areas and ripe fruit provides wine of 'fuller body'.

Even where the grape variety is constant, the style varies enormously within a climatic region. In Bordeaux, France, where a Medoc red may have a pH reading of 3.5 the sweet white table wines of Sauternes or Barsac with pH readings in excess of 3.6 will command astronomical prices ten times that of some reds. As already mentioned, a Riesling from the Rhine will be 3.1 pH yet a superb sweet red from the Duoro Valley in Portugal will be 3.6. It is of paramount importance that we aren't carried away with low figures for the sake of low figures; what we are looking for is relatively low figures.

Cool regions

Cool seasons or cold climate viticulture, as a general rule, produce grapes with naturally higher acids and lower pH readings and these wines are associated with fresher and more floral flavours. Winemakers can, and regularly do, legally adjust pH by the addition of acids, normally tartaric or sometimes citric acid.

Low pH makes numerous other valuable contributions to wine flavour and structure, including stability and prevention of spoilage. Generally, low pH inhibits bacterial spoilage (including malolactic bacteria), as most micro-organisms associated with wine have definite chemical limits for activity. For the fuller bodied Chardonnays to undergo malolactic fermentation (to produce the complex style of some New World wines), one criterion is a higher pH level, usually, but not necessarily, above 3.4.

UC Davis research

Still further, low pH wines require less SO_2 to prevent spoilage of flavour and colour. Work done at University of California, Davis, suggests that in a wine of pH 3.0, 61 per cent of the free SO2 is in molecular form but as the pH increases to 3.3, the molecular SO_2 is reduced to 3.1 per cent of the amount of the free SO2 present. The subsequent 'bound' sulphur can noticeably contribute to a lack of fruit flavour in the wine.

Acid in Mature Fruit

As fruit matures on the vine, a certain amount of chemical 'musical chairs' takes place Initially the young berry has a high content of malic acid which is retained in cool climates but respired in warm climate viticulture allowing tartaric to become the dominant acid. This respiration of malic acid decreases total acidity and increases pH. The primary fermentation (converting grape juice to wine) doesn't much alter the overall acid level. The secondary or malolactic fermentation produces lactic acid; as much as 30 per cent of malic acid is converted to lactic acid at this time.

Lactic acid is associated with milk products (from the decomposition of lactose) including cheese and, along with diacetyl, accounts for the 'buttery' and 'cheesy' descriptors sometimes given to Chardonnay wines that have undergone malolactic fermentation and, more importantly, in Cabernet Sauvignon red table wines from cool areas, that need acid reduction.

Total Acidity

Total acidity is yet another wine term that doesn't mean what it says, as it does not include carbonic acid. The term is regularly interchanged with titratable acidity, with which it is not identical; hence it becomes very confusing. Really, total acidity isn't total acidity at all, and is a term that could well be dropped. While it is still with us, the normal range of total acidity, by definition, is 5 to 7 g/l for red wines and 6 to 9 g/l for whites, measured as tartaric acid.

Titratable Acid

Titratable acid is what gives wine its acid taste—in addition to pH. Titration is a chemical process for determining, in wine, the amount of acid present and is achieved by adding sodium hydroxide to a wine sample until no more reaction takes place. The amount of titratable acid is expressed as grams per litre or percentage of volume. Tartaric acid is the standard in most of the English-speaking countries, sulphuric acid in France and Spanish-speaking countries.

Volatile Acid

Volatile acids or VA as they are more often referred to amongst the wine fraternity, can be either a plus or minus in wine quality, depending on the concentration. It is often said that some top ranking wines owe their greatness to 'controlled' amounts of VA. This is said to give them 'lift' or extra life during the smell and in-mouth evaluations. The main volatile acid is acetic acid. In a positive sense, trace amounts of VA will add a plus dimension to the wine—in larger doses it is easily detectable as a 'vinegary' character.

Acetic Exercise

Exercise #2: Adding vinegar or acetic acid with a dropper to a glass of ordinary 'jug' wine is a worthwhile exercise at home. Add a drop or two; smell and taste the wine; add a few more drops; smell and taste until the vinegar smell becomes offensive. This is a good way to learn about 'lift', 'volatility' and 'acetification'.

Acids that are steam distillable are considered volatile acids. Beside acetic acid, others found in wine are butyric, formic and propionic. Even more important, is ethyl acetate that is formed from acetic acid and ethanol and has a far lower smell threshold than acetic acid.

Historically, microbiological spoilage of wine was considered the main cause of high levels of acetic acid but in recent times it has been found that strains of certain fermentation yeasts have produced acetic acid in undesirable quantities. This is more common in white wine production methods employing low temperatures and clarified juice.

Acid Test

Exercise #3 My classes teach the discrimination of acids by the following exercise which is recommended to every wine lover. Purchase from your local home winemaker supply store or grocer (supermarket) a packet each of tartaric and citric acid. To make up a solution of each acid, mix a half teaspoon of crystals in a little warm water, then add cold water to make up a litre. Each taster needs 30–50ml of solution, so if you're going solo, two pinches will suffice in 60ml of water. You will need this amount of solution for further mixes. To determine your personal threshold, for these and other solutions, you will need four glasses. Take one half of the solution (60ml) and add an equal amount of water for mix #2 mix #1 being the base mix). Then take half of mix #2 and add an equal amount of water for mix #3. Glass 4 should be a blank water sample.

Do not keep the acid solutions overnight. Start with solution 1 and register your perceptions on the record sheet below. Rinse your mouth, preferably with distilled water, between solutions. Following a rest period, try working upwards from the blank sample until reaching the detection threshold.

Exercise #4 Another worthwhile training exercise is the triangular test-two blank samples and either sample #2 or #3. You will need an assistant to juggle the glasses around so you don't know which is the odd one or whether the odd one is solution 2 or 3. This is a first class method of learning your detection threshold and the identification and difference thresholds.

You will probably note that as a solution is diluted, the perception of the taste sensations will vary, or move from one area of the mouth to another. In my case, the strong solution of acid registers on the teeth, gums and lips; the weakest solution registers mainly on the tongue. Strong solutions of sugar and bitterness can be mouth-filling, yet the weak solutions may register on more conventional areas, the tip and rear of the tongue respectively.

Malic and lactic acids are not easy to find. Try your local home-brew shop or friendly pharmacist—but if all else fails an unripe green apple will suffice for malic acid.

You will taste in the solutions that the acid plus water mixtures are lighter in 'body' than a blank water sample. For permanent reference be sure to write down where these acids register in your mouth, or use the acid record sheet below. Although some disagree, I believe that all acids have different intensities, duration and placement. Tartaric may be noted on the top front of the tongue and leaves a sensation similar to fur on the top teeth. Citric acid may seem fresher and coarser in structure and goes half way along the top of the tongue. Some tasters think citric acid lingers longer and leaves a distinctly lemon flavour.

The hard and assertive malic acid, which has been likened to 'licking the side of a battleship', registers on the top and bottom of the tongue, and is often confused with alcohol. You may perceive malic as a green apple taste. Some students have described lactic acid, which is much softer and is often difficult to perceive, as 'cheesey' or 'buttery'.

Acid Record Chart

Record your perception of this component with an X on a scale of 10

		Weak 1 2 3	Moderate 4 5 6 7	Strong 8 9 10
Teeth	Upper	. . .	. . . .	. . .
	Lower	. . .	. . . .	. . .
Gum	Upper	. . .	. . . .	. . .
	Lower	. . .	. . . .	. . .
Lips	Upper	. . .	. . . .	. . .
	Lower	. . .	. . . .	. . .
Tongue	Tip	. . .	. . . .	. . .
	Top	. . .	. . . .	. . .
	Sides	. . .	. . . .	. . .
	Rear	. . .	. . . .	. . .
Throat		. . .	. . . .	. . .
Roof of mouth		. . .	. . . .	. . .

Acid Words

Practice these words each time you do the exercise.

Negative (Too Little)	Positive	Negative (Too Much)
Bland	Crisp	Acetic
Flat	Lively	Assertive
Flabby	Tart	Biting
Watery	Tangy	Hard
	Piquant	Pricked
	Zestful	Sour
		Sharp

MAIN ACIDS IN WINE

Organic	Origin	Comments
Citric	Grape berry	Only low quantities—dissipates during fermentation. Common in citrus fruits.
Malic	Grape berry	Prominent in most fruit and plant life. Metabolizes easily, diminishes during ripening and fermentation. Converts to lactic acid during malo-lactic fermentation. It is the 'hard' acid in green apples.

Tartaric	Grape berry	A specific grape/wine acid It is the most abundant and strongest acid in wine. If attacked by lactic bacteria it produces both lactic and volatile acidity.
Acetic	Primary ferment	Formed by acetic bacteria; also from yeasts acetic bacteria in the primary fermentation and by bacteria in malo-lactic ferments.
Lactic	Primary and Malo-	Not in grapes. Created in a lactic ferments similar manner to acetic acid during primary and malo-lactic ferments. Associated with dairy products.
Succinic	From yeast during	Not in grapes. A very stable fermentation primary fermentation acid that can be bitter.

Succinic acid has a saltier, rather than acid, taste and can be bitter at the same time.

Sugar

Amongst wine lovers, professional and students, the words sweet and sugar are often unwisely used and convey entirely wrong impressions. Many wines are sweet. The Muscat family is an example—even the driest (dry = without sugar) Muscat Epitheleum wine can appear to contain sugar, yet it is really the fruitiness of the variety that is 'mouth-filling' and will appear to register as a sugar sensation.

Such wines are suitable for diabetics and the diet conscious. For the purpose of this section sugar is defined as crystalline carbohydrates, mainly glucose and fructose. While the ratio of these sugars varies from wine to wine, it is generally considered that they exist in about equal proportions in all 'dry' wines. Both are present in many fruit juices and honey.

Diabetics

Fructose is considered to have double the sweetness of cane sugar.

Glucose, the sugar of our blood, is also present in many plants.

Glycerol and alcohols, both produced by fermenting grape sugars, are major contributors to sweetness and are discussed in the sweetness section of the tactile chapter starting on page 141.

There are exceptions that prove the rule, but it could be fairly said that all wines, regardless of their nomenclature, do contain some sugar. Brut de brut (the driest of the dry) champagne style 'bubblies' has cane sugar added. Sparkling wines labelled 'brut' may contain up to 1.5 per cent sugar by volume, 'natur' champagnes are the exceptions, having no added sugar.

Exceptions

There are two simple reasons for this sugar content in wine. The first and obvious one being that it is technically impossible to ferment all the sugar from grape juice; these are non-fermentable sugars. Secondly, the average consumer does not like naturally dry or very dry products. Brandy and sherry are other examples of naturally dry beverages that have some sweetening agent added to create a more pleasing flavour. Not only is cane sugar added to sweeten brandy but caramel (burnt sugar) is, in many cases, added to provide uniform colour in both brandy and whisky. In some cases, grape juice concentrate (jeropiga) is added to sherry as a sweetener.

Residual Sugar

Amongst wine lovers, professional and beginner, the words sweet and sugar are often unwisely used and convey entirely wrong impressions. Many wines are considered 'sweet'—Pinot noir and Grenache are examples of wines that are sweet but have no residual sugar.

Modern technology allows the winemaker scope to control the amount of natural grape sugar left in the wine during fermentation. Any amount retained is called residual sugar. It is important for communication and a clear understanding that we are positive about the terms residual and non-fermentable.

Dryness is a comparative term but in white table wines sugar begins to be perceivable at about 0.4 per cent by volume. In red wines the sugar level needs to reach about 1.5 per cent because of the masking effect of tannins. The balance of sugar and acid is vital in sensory evaluation as high sugar or acid levels tend to hide each other, in addition to fatiguing the sense receptors.

Some winemakers are experimenting with late harvest (high sugar) red table wines by not fully completing the primary fermentation, thereby leaving some residual sugar in the finished red wine. This revolutionary approach flies in the face of conventional dry red table wine; but why must we always have dry red table wines?

Our modern cuisine is far removed from the food styles that traditionally accompanied dry reds. Sugar gives wine body as well as sweetness and many of us know dishes that scream out for a full bodied, slightly sweet red. Lambrusco, that slightly effervescent and sweet, north Italian red wine, surely must rank as one of the world's most popular wines, so, who is the 'authority' that dictates that we can't have medium to full bodied sweet red table wines? That all time American favorite 'hearty burgundy', also happens to have one to two per cent residual sugar.

If a wine lover doesn't like this style there's no obligation to drink it. One thing is sure, he or she is not going to learn anything from ignoring the style, or from summary dismissal.

Many of the world's great sweet white table wines evolved in Germany, considered the home of the Riesling wine style and originally, Traminer (Gewurz) as well. Incidentally, Alsace, France is now considered the centre for Traminer. But Germany, like the Champagne region, is the northern limit where grapes will ripen and seasons vary widely. While lesser wine categories like Tafelwein, Qualitatswein bestimmter Anbaugebiet (QbA) may have sugar

**German
standards**

added to the fermentation (a process called chapitalisation). The Qualitatswein mit Pradikat (QmP = wines with special attributes) classification forbids this practice.

The QmP classifications are: Kabinett, Spatlese, Auslese, Beerenauslese and Trockenbeerenalese. To qualify for these titles, the German Wine Laws of 1971 require that the 'must' contains a minimum amount of natural sugar. The measurement is known as Ochsle (pronounced Erks-la) for the nineteenth century founder of the scale, Ferdinand Ochsle. Briefly, Ochsle relates to specific gravity. The following table for the Rheingau, one of the 11 pronounced German wine regions, is indicative of standards of Ochsle required for QmP wines made from the Riesling grape variety: Kabinett-73, Spatlese-85, Auslese-95, Beerenauslese-125, Trocken-beeren-auslese-150.

MUST CONVERSION CHART

SPECIFIC GRAVITY	OCHSLE (GERMAN)	BAUMÉ (AUST)	BRIX (USA/NZ)	APPROX % ALCOHOL (V/V)
1.070	70	9.4	17.0	8.8
1.075	75	10.1	18.1	9.4
1.080	80	10.7	19.3	10.0
1.085	85	11.3	20.4	10.6
1090	90	11.9	21.5	11.3
1.095	95	12.5	22.5	11.9
1.100	100	13.1	23.7	12.5
1.105	105	13.7	24.8	13.1
1.110	110	14.3	25.8	13.8

There are individual standards for all 11 German wine regions, and for all varieties including red and white grapes.

The grape varieties Riesling, (Gewurz) Traminer and Muscat are closely related, particularly in fragrance, and are considered to be aromatic varieties. Much of their highly 'floral' aroma comes from the terpine alcohols linalool, nerol and geraniol. These highly scented wines appear to be unbalanced if made in the naturally dry style (when all grape sugar is converted to alcohol) and most winemakers agree that these wines benefit from some residual sugar to give the wine balance of flavour and body.

While there are many superb sweet white table wines made in Canada, Australia, New Zealand and other wine producing nations, the benchmarks are from the French regions of Barsac and Sauternes (made from the grape varieties Semillon and Sauvignon), the Hungarian style Tokay made with Furmint grapes and the German styles mentioned above.

Sugar Exercises

Exercise #5 Make up sugar and water solutions by adding a heaped dessertspoon of sugar to a glass of water. Then make up the three mixes and the blank water sample as explained under acids on page 123. Write on your record sheet where the sugar registers in the mouth. Observe the difference in the viscosity or 'body' of the number one solution. Note how it lies in your mouth, rather limply and has a 'cloying' finish.

Now you are ready for a triangular test with the sugar solutions.

Combine equal amounts of the number one tartaric acid and water solution with the number one sugar and water solution and see how acid brings the solution to 'life', lightens the 'body' and makes the finish much crisper by removing the 'cloying' nature of the sugar. The sugar solution gives viscosity or 'body' to the acid and water solution.

Sugar Words   Practice these words each time you do the exercise.

Negative (Too Little)	**Positive**	**Negative** (Too Much)
Lacking	Sweet	Syrupy
Watery	Semi-sweet	Cloying
Thin	Semi-dry	
	Balanced	

SUGAR RECORD CHART

Record your perception of this component with an X on a scale of 10 (mark with x)

		Weak 1 2 3	Moderate 4 5 6 7	Strong 8 9 10
Teeth	**Upper**	. . .	. . . .	. . .
	Lower	. . .	. . . .	. . .
Gums	**Upper**	. . .	. . . .	. . .
	Lower	. . .	. . . .	. . .
Lips	**Upper**	. . .	. . . .	. . .
	Lower	. . .	. . . .	. . .
Tongue	**Tip**	. . .	. . . .	. . .
	Top	. . .	. . . .	. . .
	Sides	. . .	. . . .	. . .
	Rear	. . .	. . . .	. . .
Throat		. . .	. . . .	. . .
Roof of mouth		. . .	. . . .	. . .

SUGAR/ACID MIX RECORD CHART

Record your perception of these components on a scale of 10

		Weak	Moderate	Strong
		1 2 3	4 5 6 7	8 9 10
Teeth	Upper	. . .	. . . .	. . .
	Lower	. . .	. . . .	. . .
Gums	Upper	. . .	. . . .	. . .
	Lower	. . .	. . . .	. . .
Lips	Upper	. . .	. . . .	. . .
	Lower	. . .	. . . .	. . .
Tongue	Tip	. . .	. . . .	. . .
	Top	. . .	. . . .	. . .
	Sides	. . .	. . . .	. . .
Cheeks	Front	. . .	. . . .	. . .
	Rear	. . .	. . . .	. . .
Throat		. . .	. . . .	. . .
Roof of mouth		. . .	. . . .	. . .

Bitterness

Bitter
salts

Historically, humans and animals have been well served by nature as nearly all poisonous food plants, berries and roots are bitter. Excessive bitterness is possibly the most universally disliked component of all foods and beverages. Bitterness in food and beverages comes from two sources: vegetable extracts and chemical salts. The vegetable extracts are: cassia, gentian, quinquina and nux vomica. Potassium iodide, potassium sulfate, sodium iodide, magnesium chloride, calcium chloride and quinine sulfate are some of the salts providing bitterness.

During bacterial decomposition, glycerin becomes acrolein and by combining with the polyphenols becomes bitter. Yet, as a basic taste response even the sweetest wine should have some bitterness, even if it is below the perceivable threshold—just as the driest wine will have sugar, also below perceptability. It's my strong belief that nearly all food and beverages should contain a measurable amount of each of the five basic tastes to provide balance and complexity. The subject is further discussed with astringency in the tactile chapter.

Over the years the word 'bitter' has been synonymous with lager and ale. Maybe these brewed beverages are bitter. To my personal taste most US and Australian beers are decidedly sweet in the mouth, with an unpleasant bitter aftertaste. Maybe my perceptions are fooling me, but, the sweetness level of beer has apparently increased considerably in the past decade—or is it that I do not like sweet beverages? I think not, as I have an intense love of sweet table and fortified wines.

Strong black coffee, tea, tonic water and soluble aspirin are everyday examples of bitterness. For the majority of people bitterness and astringency are an acquired taste. On the positive side bitterness does have an important role (albeit that of a poor relative) in many wine styles, particularly dry reds and the drier fortified wines.

Bitterness, in wine, is a product of phenolic extractions (along with colour) from the grape skins, seeds and stems. This also contributes to astringency. As such, bitterness is born in the first week of the wine's life—from the first moment the grapes are 'damaged' either by mechanical harvesting or by being crushed at the winery.

As winemaking and associated grape harvesting methods differ enormously between large and small producers, it is impossible to come out in favor of any particular technique. While many producers around the world pick one bunch of grapes at a time, an increasing number are using several mechanical harvesters turning in 30 tons an hour. Both methods of harvesting can have a dramatic impact on bitterness.

Mechanical harvesters

Most grapes in the Northern Hemisphere are picked in the autumn although some are harvested as early as July, others not until November. Hot weather and travel, have a definite influence on high berry/must temperature. This is the very essence of increased pH and phenolic extraction and bitterness as demonstrated by a sample of grapes tested in Missouri: at 48°F = pH 3.20; at 59°F = pH 3.37; at 66°F = pH 3.45; at 80°F the pH was 3.47.

The small grape vineyardist has several methods to combat these problems and, fortunately, so has the larger producer. Unlike human grape pickers, mechanical grape harvesters can, and do, work through the cool night hours. So much so that a leading Californian sparkling wine producer with a specialist interest in premium wine quality, has come out in favour of the mechanical method; a decision not reached lightly.

Bitterness Exercise

Make up a bitter solution by doubling the strength of your normal cup of tea or coffee—doesn't the thought make you shudder? If you can obtain 50 mg of quinine sulfate from your friendly pharmacist, mix it with four ounces of water and that is the same bitter mix used in laboratory tests.

Bitterness exercise

UMAMI

You probably know about the four generally accepted basic taste sensations—sweet, sour, salt and bitter—but what about the fifth one—umami? (ooo-mom-eee). This ancient Japanese taste sensation is difficult to translate into any other language, but for the want of a better English word, deliciousness has made its way into the textbooks of taste sensations and pleasure. Umami also has connotations of being savoury.

I have always had problems with *sweetness* as a taste sense because there are many things in wine that are sweet—but they are not sugar. For instance, many wines are sweet but have no measurable amounts of fermentable sugars; I can only repeat that Pinot noir and Grenache are wonderful examples of this. It is my opinion that if Pinot noir (black) is not sweet, it's not Pinot. Yet, this does not apply to either Pinot gris (grey) or Pinot blanc (white) that have no sweetness when compared to Pinot noir, from which they mutated.

Sugar & sweetness

What I am saying is that *sugar* is the taste sense, rather than *sweetness*. Other wine components such as oak, fruit flavours, glycerol and alcohol can be sweet, yet they are not *taste* sensations; are they a separate category like umami? Very simply, we do not know. This is a very inexact science that is completely upset when people talk about getting wine on their palate? What does this mean—where is the palate?

What then is umami? Some foods have a distinctive, enjoyable, yet indefinable flavour and taste; that's umami.

The worst thing about umami is that a Japanese scientist who was enamoured with its flavour, discovered it in the very early years of the last millennium. He found that its source was what was to become America's dreaded glutamate. Of course, Americans didn't know anything about Japanese food—or what glutamate was in those years.

Sensory research shows that glutamate does not enhance any of the four basic tastes, nor can the umami taste be formed by any combination of the classic four.

Despite glutamate's clean bill of health from the USAs Food and Drug Administration (FDA), years later the nation's mischievous media caused yet another panic amongst the population by telling us how bad MSG (monosodium glutamate) was for our health. According to them it caused hot flushes in the kitchen sink, in-grown toe nails in elephants, partial deafness in your left foot's ear, and even ageing women had their hair turn red instead of silver!

MSG

Restaurants the world over had to display notices NO MSG USED HERE even though they did use it in the form of soya sauce which is a ready supply of MSG—because the chefs knew of its great flavor value. In one Australian state (NSW) harsh laws against the use of MSG have come into use to protect the population from something that is scientifically inoffensive.

Umami

Where does one find umami? How does one recognize it? When you bite into a fresh, (it must be fresh) peach or tomato—or almost any other fully ripe fruit or vegetable where the flavour is irresistible—that's umami. But don't expect it from supermarket fruit. Those are only a few of a thousand examples—almost any meat or seafood that is delicious—that's umami.

Some other examples of where umami can be found are sun-dried tomatoes or shitake mushrooms, and ham and other cured and aged meats. At home we make a umami Catalan savoury fish pate from anchovies and black olives.

One group particularly suited to the task of educating the public is food editors who put their senses to work during an International Food Information Council sponsored workshop 'Savor the Flavor in Food,' during the International Food Media Conference in Orlando, Florida.

Food media conferees were challenged to identify the umami taste provided by glutamate in one of three samples of chicken stock. The samples were all prepared from the same basic recipe using chicken parts and vegetables, varying only in the presence or absence of salt and MSG.

In terms of taste preferences 75 percent of the editors indicated they preferred the broth with the umami flavour contributed by glutamate. They described the taste as 'rich,' 'well-rounded,' 'savoury,' 'full-bodied,' 'brothy,' and 'more chicken-like.'

Glutamate is an amino acid that is found throughout the human body. It is also naturally present in protein-rich foods such as cheese, meat, fish and human milk. When present in its 'free' form in foods, not bound together with other amino acids in protein, glutamate exerts its umami-flavour effect.

MSG added to foods provides a similar flavouring function as the 'free' glutamate that occurs naturally in foods. It is often used to flavour meats, poultry, seafood, soups, stews, sauces and gravies.

Thirty-eight percent of the editors mistakenly identified the salt-only chicken stock as the one containing MSG. Although many people have the misperception that MSG makes food taste saltier, MSG contains only one-third the amount of sodium as table salt. MSG can be used in many foods to reduce the total amount of sodium by 20 to 40 percent, while maintaining an acceptable flavour.

MSG

MSG is classified by the Food and Drug Administration as a Generally Recognized as Safe (GRAS) substance. All foods with added MSG must list the ingredient on the label as monosodium glutamate.

'Having experienced the umami taste sensation first-hand, hopefully food editors can help educate consumers about MSG's unique and flavourful contribution to foods,' said Susan Schiffman Ph.D., professor of medical psychology and director of the weight loss clinic at Duke University Medical Center.

In conducting clinical research on persons with taste and smell impairments, Schiffman also has found that many consumers mistakenly believe MSG is a preservative or meat tenderiser.

As mentioned earlier, when an apple is turned into juice, crushed or stewed so it changes its flavour; these changes also increase or decrease the amount of umami. This applies equally to the ripening of fruit whether it be anything from tomatoes to grapes; ripe fruit has more flavour-laden umami.

Strangely, ageing, drying, and fermentation all increase the umami level of food; even cheese and soya sauce come into this category.

Ripe fruit

It is said that fully ripened tomatoes have 10 times more umami than unripe tomatoes. Much of the success of Australian wines in the international markets is the umami flavour in the intensely ripe Syrah/Shiraz wines. The fermentation process also gives condiments like Worcestershire sauce, Bovril (beef tea) and Vegemite *q.v.*, loads of umami flavour. Combine any of these with aged beef and you have a meal just bursting with umami flavour. Vegetarians can also enjoy umami flavours through fresh ripe vegetables.

HEAT SUMMATION

This book deliberately endeavoured to keep away from the technical aspect of viticulture and winemaking. Yet if the wine lover is to reach her or his full potential as a judge of wine, there are some matters of viticulture and oenology that should be understood.

The following reprint from my book *Wine is Fun!* (International Wine Academy Publications) ISBN 0 9596983 0 7 covers the subject of heat summation and provides an understanding of the part played by climate and geography which is pertinent to this chapter. *(Wine is Fun!* also covers soil, winemaking, wine styles, grapes, oak barrels and more basic material.)

Heat summation is the standard technique used in comparing and assessing the almost infinite permutations of climatic and geographical features that make up any wine appellation/region. Basically it is a way of ensuring one of the most critical elements of viticulture—the amount of heat and sunshine involved in the growing and ripening processes of the fruit. Vines don't like being too close to the Equator or the Poles. Other than these obvious points of latitude, there are three major factors affecting the amount of heat provided to the vines: water, soil and elevation.

Bodies of Water

Critical elements

Many of the classical wine areas are on slopes close to large bodies of water, which store heat during the day and release it at night thus giving the vines a desirable evenness of temperature. One thinks of Germany's Rhine Valley, France's Valley of the Marne, or of Bordeaux, between the Atlantic Ocean and the Gironde River. Canadian winegrowers around Lake Erie and others near the Finger Lakes of New York State, and the regions bordering Lake Erie, are very conscious of the impact of these large water bodies in equalizing temperatures. (Many Californian regions have a maritime influence, particularly the ones where, almost daily, fogs roll in from the Pacific.) This factor is of little importance in Australia, where, except for vines along the Murray River and a few in Victoria, Tasmania, NSW and Western Australia, most vines are well removed from any large lakes or rivers.

Soil

A second factor affecting the vines *micro*-climate (within a metre of the vine) is stony soil, which, like water bodies, stores heat during the day and thus contributes to diurnal evenness between day and night temperatures.

Elevation

The third factor is elevation. Obviously, the higher we go above sea level the cooler the climate. Many of Australia's vineyards are situated around the Great Dividing Range that forms the spine of the eastern states, from northern Queensland to Great Western in Victoria, in much the same way as the Appalachians spear down the eastern side of the United States. The stunning mountains of South Africa's main wine regions contribute greatly to their wines.

Vineyard Siting

After sleeping all winter the vines come to life with the first flush of spring warmth, when the temperature reaches a mean daily average of 10°C (50°F). Depending on the heat summation and the grape variety, the new fruit will be ready for harvesting anytime from 90 to 190 days after budburst. This is a great range of harvest seasons, especially when some areas have only 120 days of frost-free growing time. Thus it is vital that vignerons have the right varieties planted in the right areas (particularly when, in Australia and the USA, they have a minimum of 80 varieties to choose from).

They are helped in this decision by a valuable guide to vineyard selection developed by researchers at the University of California, Davis. The technique is called 'heat summation' and is obtained by totalling the number of degrees above a mean of 50°F (10°C) for each day of the growing season. In the Southern Hemisphere, this period is from October 1 to April 30.

In the Northern Hemisphere the period covers April 1 to October 30. Thus if the temperature today is 80°F we deduct 50 and have 30 heat units for the day. These heat units are added for each day of the growing season to arrive at the heat summation. Grapes need a minimum of 1700 such units to have any chance of ripening, and a maximum of 5200 units.

The viticultural areas of the world have been classified into five levels of heat summation. Australia and North America are represented in all five. Some comparative examples will quickly suggest the wide viticultural (and therefore winemaking) choices available in these countries.

Regions one and two are ideally suited to making light dry table wines of distinction as the fruit ripens late in the season allowing maximum flavour build up. In the warmer region three, fruit fully ripens earlier providing wines with more body.

Measuring heat

While others think differently, some think that grapes maturing quickly produce wines suitable only for drinking at a young age (including a lot of bulk wines for jugs and casks). These wines come from warmer area regions four and five that are also known for their excellent ports and brandies.

All this is generalization, as the most expensive sweet table wines come from regions one and two, and some splendid and expensive table wines come from regions four and five. Consequently, critics of the degree day heat measurement scheme say that it is inaccurate. But it was only ever meant to be a guide and one of the many factors to be considered in vineyard site selection.

IN-MOUTH PROFILES

Not only do we have a need for an hedonic point score, we also need to determine what makes one Riesling, Chardonnay or Syrah different to other wines in the flight. ('Flight'—a group of wines, normally six, presented for evaluation.)

This in-mouth profiling is the first simple step. Later in our work we will combine olfactory and in-mouth profiling.

Sugar not applicable

Each 'spoke' of the wheel represents a scale of 1–10, one being nearest the centre and representing low intensity. Ten is on the outside of the spoke and represents high intensity.

Wine No 1 profile below: Sugar not applicable to this red wine style. Young (2–3 years old), cool climate, region 1–2, dry red. High acid, medium oak, high grape tannin, moderate to high alcohol, dormant fruit. Reasonably high alcohol and tannin gives high viscosity, balance just above moderate due to high acid, alcohol and low fruit. As this wine develops with bottle maturation (evolution) the latent fruit will be enhanced and the other components will combine to give the wine good balance. Because of its good fruit, acid and tannin, this wine is a good long term cellaring prospect, more than eight years from vintage date. Start by placing an X on the level you think is appropriate on the vector and then join the Xs.

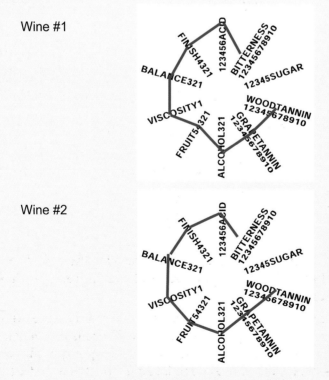

Wine #1

Wine #2

Wine No 2: Regions 3–4, dry red 3–4 years old. Less acid, touch more oak as the winemaker believed the ripe fruit could hold more. At this time a better balanced wine than No 1 and softer finish. Good medium term cellaring wine, 5-8 years from vintage date.

Wine No 3: Top class aged dry red from regions 1–3, say 8–10 years old. Approaching its peak, with a long time to run. Shows all the benefits of evolution in a good cellar; everything in balance.

Wine No 4: A badly made wine using poor quality grapes.

By carefully recording your impressions on the profiles we are able, at a glance, to tell why these wines are different, even though they were made from the same variety. This is a good method to highlight the differing viticultural and vinification methods when comparing wines from within one appellation.

Why different?

Lowest intensity on the 10 point scale is nearest the centre. One method of using the scale is to consider an average wine as being 5/10, a wine lacking in, say acid, that was 'watery' would be less than 5, one that is high in acid 'crisp/biting' would range from 6–10. Start with the acid component. When you have considered the intensity of that component, mark that number or

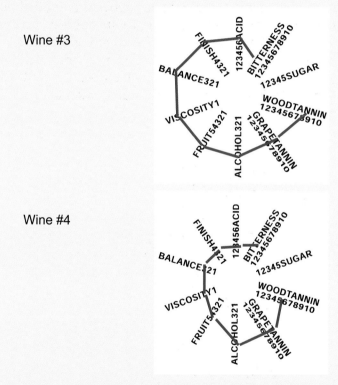

Wine #3

Wine #4

letter with an X and move onto the next component marking them with an X. By linking each X together, we have a graphic profile of your perceptions—and a disciplined approach to evaluation.

We are endeavouring to make a rounded circle. A low viscosity wine might have all troughs, the wine will rate poorly for balance. That may or may not be a problem. A young red wine rating excessive wood and grape tannins but with obvious fruit has good potential. A wine lacking fruit has no future. It is a most interesting exercise comparing your *In Mouth profiles* with others in your group. Do not forget to complete the profiles every time you are seriously critiquing wine. It will ensure that you focus on the essentials points of wine evaluation, and you will quickly elevate your skills.

SOME TASTY WORDS

Oral Cavity	The mouth.
Flavour Impression	A combination of smell, taste and temperature/texture from the touch sense.
Papillae	The taste receptors on the rough surface of the tongue containing taste cells.
Physiology	The science of essential life processes.
Sapid	Substances that have taste.
Threshold	The intensity below which a stimulus cannot be perceived and can produce no response.
Vegemite®/Marmite®	Australian vegetable extract spread. Used mainly for spreading on toast at breakfast or children's sandwiches.
Volatile Acids	Acids that are steam distillable—acetic, butyric, formic, and propionic that do have aroma.

TASTE SUMMARY

- The sense of taste is a very limited sense that covers only the perception of sugar, sour, salt umami, and bitter. Each and every individual has a different threshold for these components.
- When we have a common cold we lose our sense of smell. Taste is rarely affected.
- Our taste buds are replaced at about weekly intervals.
- There are no general groupings for the basic taste sensations of acid (sour), sugar and salt. These can be perceived with equal sensitivity all over the mouth. However, it does vary from one individual to another. Bitterness is most pronounced at the rear of the mouth.
- Learn to discriminate the difference between *sugar* and *sweetness*.
- Bitterness and astringency, in detectable quantities, are essential components of taste and flavour in young red wines.
- Sapid substances are those having taste.
- Glycerol and alcohols, both produced by fermenting grape sugars, are major contributors to sweetness.

TASTE MADE EASY

1. Firstly, we have two palates—the soft and hard palates. Secondly, the soft palate at the rear of the mouth does perceive taste; most scientists say that the hard palate, or the roof of the mouth, has no taste receptors in which case how can it have anything to with the sense of taste?

2. Bear in mind that *taste* and *flavour* are formed in the

, then relayed to the mouth. The brain, at the same time, is considering smell and combining it with taste to provide you with the overall flavour impression. Concentration at this time will help enormously in forming a worthwhile opinion.

3. It is of prime concern to the budding sensory evaluator/judge that taste is recognized for what it is—a very limited sense; and our efforts should be concentrated in the discrimination of the overall flavor impressions—taste, smell and the two other components: *temperature* and *texture.*

4. In fact, we don't taste flavour in our mouth, we actually perceive the signals and then assemble them all together, make decisions such as 'I like' or 'I do not like' *in the brain*, and then these messages are relayed back to the mouth

5. Acid gives wine *life* and *freshness*, sugar contributes to *viscosity*. Wines with high acidity and low pH are likely to be better cellaring wines, consistent with the other factors of flavour being present.

6. Bitterness and astringency, in detectable quantities, are essential components of taste and flavour in young red wines.

7. It is impossible to over-emphasise how differently that each of us perceives the same stimulus and the strength we perceive that stimulus. Every person alive has a different threshold for each of the senses, in other words we are not all the same as many wine 'experts' would have us believe.

9. The lack of knowledge, the difficulty in measuring taste responses (even trained people can only give about 40 per cent accurate response) and the difference between animals used in laboratory tests and human subjects, makes for a lack of positive statements about the taste sense.

10. Taste buds contain 50–100 taste cells with finger-like microvilli protruding from each cell and these poke through the taste pore at the top of the taste bud. So, we have taste *buds*, taste *cells* and taste *pores* all working to respond to our eating and drinking.

11 The mouth is host to three sensations: taste, smell and touch. When we eat or drink, what are known as tastants enter our mouth, these are the chemicals in that food or drink and they become associated with our saliva. These various chemicals instantly find their way onto the taste cells and through an amazing series of connections register in the brain.

12. There are also non-volatile and volatile acids. The natural fruit acids—malic, tartaric and citric are non-volatile, while those produced during fermentation such as lactic, acetic, succinic, formic, propionic are volatile.

A completed Wine Evaluation Record

WINE DETAILS		SIGHT 4 max	AROMA/ BOUQUET 6 max	IN MOUTH 6 max	AFTER FLAVOUR 2 max	OVERALL 2 max	TOTAL 20 max
1	Vintage '01 Cullen Variety Chardonnay Region Margaret River WA	4	5.25	5.50	2	1.75	18.50
	Comments Light gold colour–brilliant appearance, barrel-fermented, big on aromas of stone fruits and a little citrus. In-mouth the oaky flavours merge well with the good fruit. Stunning length and excellent finish						
2	Vintage '01 Bouchard Pere Variety Chardonnay Region Le Montrachet	3.5	4.75	4.75	1.75	1.50	16.25
	Comments Light straw colour–bright appearance, some melon & fig aromas, no apparent oak. medium after-flavour, bit short on complexity. Clean finish—just a little bitter.						
3	Vintage '01 Robert Mondavi Variety Chardonnay Region Napa CA	3.75	5.25	5.25	1.75	1.75	17.75
	Comments Golden colour–appearance star bright. a wine with great promise, complex tropical fruits on nose—oak well balanced; has bracing, fresh mouth-feel and good length.						
4	Vintage '01 Hamilton-Russel Variety Chardonnay Region Walker Bay, S.Af	4	5.25	5.25	1.75	1.75	18
	Comments Medium straw colour–brilliant appearance; bold style with some pear, tropical fruit & mineral aromas; citrus, melon and butterscotch aromas—good oak balance. Crisp and excellent finish						
5	Vintage '01 Floating Mtn Variety Chardonnay Region Waipara NZ	4	5.50	5.50	2	1.75	18.75
	Comments Light golden colour–appearance star-bright. Definitive citrus-pear-green apple, cold climate aromas. Tons of fruit, supported by MLF butteriness. A smart wine—long after-flavour, drink now or better in 4-5 years.						

IN MOUTH

6 points	Extraordinary	Unmistakable characteristic flavour of a grape variety or wine type. Extraordinary balance. Smooth, full bodied, mouth filling and over whelming.
5 points	Excellent	All of the above but a little less. Excellent but not overwhelming.
4 points	Good	Characteristic grape variety or wine type flavour. Good balance. Smooth. May have minor faults. Good wine.
3 points	Pleasant	Undistinguished wine but pleasant.
2 points	Acceptable	Undistinguished wine with minor imperfections and/or more pronounced faults than 5, 4 or 3 above.
1 point	Poor	Offensive flavours. May be drinkable with strong foods.
0 points	Objectionable	Undrinkable.

AFTER-FLAVOUR

2 points	Excellent	A chance to reward an excellent wine.
1 point	Good	
0 points	Poor	

OVERALL

2 points	Excellent	Lingering, outstanding after-flavour.
1 point	Good	Pleasant after-flavour.
0 points	Poor	Little or no distinguishable after-flavour.

CHAPTER 7

Either we want to live or we want to die, and while we are alive we surely want to live more abundantly, to our potential, to release our capacities, instead of living a death in life. We cannot be fully alive if our feelings are dead.

—R.D. Laing, Sensory Processes

TACTILE—TOUCH

Some years ago, three happily-married, middle-aged ladies came to one of my New York seminars and I was surprised to learn that they were all teetotallers. Imagine my surprise when they turned-up for a second and even a third seminar. On their second visit I enquired as to why they had returned and the immediate reply was that they had learnt so much about touch and feel that their cooking had improve significantly.

So what is said in the following chapter applies equally to food as it does to wine. In fact, I have gone right inside the food business to explain the intricacies of this profound subject.

At the University of Western Sydney we have Australia's oldest food science school that is resplendent with the best equipment in the food sciences business, including a production winery. The equipment includes a tongue laboratory, spectrophotometer and viscometer discussed under viscosity.

The sense of touch shows us the shape, size and *feel* of our world. The sense of touch is also the main difference, other than colour, between red and white wine. When given a white wine with red food colouring, almost everybody scores the wine as a red wine. This is a good measure of how important touch is in the overall evaluation of wine.

Discussing the helpful aspects of this sense leads us down many interesting pathways. We are kept *safe* by learning to avoid touching a burner or a flame, a sharp edge or point, very cold metal. Our feelings are *happy* when we stroke a dog, when we get a hug, when… so many other things.

Our feelings are *sad* when we run into something hard or cut our finger. We wonder why we itch and why scratching that itchy nose relieves it.

The *tickling* conundrum is simply in a class of its own. Why does tickling make us laugh? Why are certain parts more ticklish than others? Why can't we tickle ourselves? Why is tickling funny for only so long, then it makes us peevish?

Think about your feet in wet grass—or on the hot sand of a beach. Or the sharp prick of a needle, and the shooting pain when you bang your elbow. Without a sense of touch, all those experiences would feel pretty much the same.

Thousands of receptors for touch work together to help provide the brain with information about the outside world. Sometimes, a touch is noxious and offensive, and is identified by specialized receptors as a source of pain. Regardless of whether a touch is good or bad, a signal travels from sensors in the skin through nerves to the spinal cord and the brain, where it is decoded and interpreted.

Our feelings

Top equipment

Tickling?

The dictionary gives us a simplistic definition of the tactile sense: 'of perceived by, connected with the sense of touch'. The *tactile* sense is the ability to sense texture and pressure by touch. According to Webster, touch is 'the special sense by which pressure or traction exerted on the skin or mucous membrane is perceived.'

The tactile sense indicates what something feels like, where on your body you feel it, and how much you feel it.

Unfortunate

Unfortunately, the international wine industry has been so involved in the numbers game about the amounts of acid, sugar and alcohol which instruments can measure, that many other important issues such as flavour have been overlooked. A small number of forward looking wineries and research institutes are the rare exceptions. However, it is fair to say that the 21st century has brought a new interest in the tactile sense, often referred to very loosely, and incorrectly, as *mouth feel* only.

When we use such common wine descriptions such as bubbly, sparkling, creamy, light/full body, rough, smooth, round, velvety, coarse, thin, hot, peppery, to list a few, we are referring not to the taste but rather the tactile and temperature senses—and mainly the *textural* aspect of the touch sense.

PHYSIOLOGY OF TOUCH

Specific exteroreceptors for pain, touch, pressure, heat and cold are located in the skin. These receptors are most numerous in areas such as the fingertips, palms and lips; they are more sparsely distributed elsewhere in the body.

Where?

The skin of our body contains many different nerve endings that carry the various receptors. Those that interest us in food and beverage evaluation are:

- **thermoreceptors**—heat and cold.
- **nociceptors**—which detect painful stimulations such as pin prick or extremes of cold and heat.
- **mechanoreceptors**—pressure (some instant, some continuous).

Nearest the surface of the skin are the free nerve endings that register pain, coldness and continuous touch. A little deeper are touch and pressure receptors. Deeper still are the heat receptors and nerve endings that monitor movement affecting the hair follicles.

All sensory information goes to the egg-shaped *thalamus* in the middle of the brain. The thalamus, a type of clearing house, sorts information and directs it to the primary *somatosensory cortex* (surface of the brain) which receives tactile information, pain, pressure, position, movement and temperature.

Different parts of the *cortex* (see The Brain pages 83–85) receives information from each set of sense organs; these areas cover the brain like segments of an orange—the segments are proportionate to the importance of the sense.

Smell and taste areas are small, but touch covers a wide band across the brain where sensitive parts of our body such as the hands and the lips take up a large part of the cortex.

The sensitivity of the skin varies in different parts of the body—high sensitivity on the tip of the tongue, lips and tips of the fingers—low sensitivity on the back of the hands. As with our other senses—sight, hearing and smell, we all have a personal threshold for each touch sense.

Our body will monitor the environment in which we live, be it Alaska or Algeria, and adjust our thermal requirements. Sports persons and soldiers learn to absorb high levels of pain, while surgeons, masseurs, artists and the like, learn the art of delicate touch.

To say the very least, what is happening in the science world regarding our brain and our tactile sense is absolutely amazing and one wonders what the situation will be in only one future decade? Here follows a fascinating story of what is ahead of us.

Scientists used a stimulation technique to improve the sensitivity of people's fingertips, then gave them drugs that either doubled or deleted this effect. Similar skin stimulation/drug treatment combinations may eventually help the elderly or stroke victims button shirts and aid professional pianists according to Dr. Hubert Dinse, author of a paper that appeared in the journal *Science* of the American Association for Advancement of Science.

Fascinating story

Finger stimulations and drugs can temporarily reorganize parts of the human brain. This stimulation, called co-activation, shuffles the synapses that link neurons. The stimulated area becomes more sensitive as more neurons are recruited to process encountered tactile information. The scientists showed that amphetamine doubled stimulation-induced gains in tactile acuity. In the presence of an alternate drug, an NMDA blocker, the improvements in tactile acuity, or perceptual learning, gained via finger stimulations were lost.

Dr. Hubert Dinse said that related treatments could improve a person's ability to read Braille and that drug-mediated muscle stimulation could help the elderly and chronic pain patients perform everyday tasks.

'We are at the beginning of an era where we can interact with the brain. We can apply what we know about brain plasticity to train it to alter behavior. People are always trying to find ways to improve learning. What we tested is unconscious skill learning. How far could this carry to cognitive learning?… that remains to be seen,' said Dinse.

'My personal opinion,' Dinse maintained, 'is that progress in brain pharmacology will sooner or later result in implications that are equally or possibly more dramatic than the implications tied to discussions about genes and cloning.'

One can only ask the good doctor, 'when will we all be able to turn on an automatic and perfect wine tasting mouth?'

NERVES

Having reached this stage of the book, the time has arrived for the serious student to have a closer look at how we see, smell, taste and feel wine. A little understanding of how these things happen is easy with a determined study effort—and is very useful information.

Three nervous systems serve the face and mouth for perception of texture.

Cranial nerve #5 trigeminal: which has free nerve endings. Sensory effects: teeth, oral mucosa—*(membrane lining all body passages that communicate with the air, such as the respiratory and alimentary tracts, and having cells and associated glands that secrete mucus),* nasal mucosa, eye and general sensory effects in the front two thirds of the tongue.

Cranial nerve #7 parasympathetic: (conservation and replenishment of bodily resources – contraction and secretion) glands of mouth, nose, hard palate, eye, lower jaw and under the tongue

Cranial nerve #9 trigeminal (tri-jem-in-al): nerve is the largest of the cranial nerves and has three main branches, the *ophthalmic (eyes-nose)*, *maxillary* (upper jaw), and *mandibular* (lower jaw).

The sensory portion of cranial nerve #5, contained in the *ophthalmic* branch, for our purposes, conveys information from the skin of the nasal cavity, side of the nose, forehead, and the anterior (front) half of the skull.

Sensory fibres in the *maxillary* branch come from the mucosa of the nose, hard palate, parts of the pharynx, upper teeth, upper lip and lower eyelid.

The sensory fibres of the *mandibular* branch originate from the front two-thirds of the tongue, lower teeth, skin over the lower jaw, the cheek and mucosa, and the side of the head anterior to the ear.

Each branch of the trigeminal nerve conveys the somatosensory (so-mat-o-sen-sory) *sensations* of touch, pain, and temperature.

The **somatosensory system** includes multiple types of sensation from the body—light touch, pain, pressure, temperature, and other muscle function

However, these modalities (any of the various types of sensation, such as touch, sight or hearing) are lumped into three different pathways in the spinal cord and have different targets in the brain. The first modality is called **discriminative touch**, which includes touch, pressure, and vibration perception, and enables us to "read" raised letters with our fingertips, or describe the shape and texture of an object without seeing it.

The second grouping is **pain and temperature**, and also includes the sensations of itch and tickle.

These modalities differ in their receptors, pathways, targets, and also in the level of crossing. Any sensory system going to the cerebral cortex will have to cross over hemispheres at some point, because the cerebral cortex operates on a contralateral (opposite side) basis. The discriminative touch system crosses *high*—in the medulla. The pain system crosses *low*—in the spinal cord. The proprioceptive system is going to the cerebellum, which works ipsilaterally (same side). Therefore this system doesn't cross.

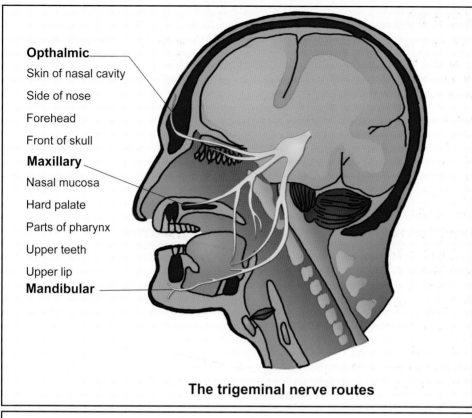

Opthalmic
- Skin of nasal cavity
- Side of nose
- Forehead
- Front of skull

Maxillary
- Nasal mucosa
- Hard palate
- Parts of pharynx
- Upper teeth
- Upper lip

Mandibular

The trigeminal nerve routes

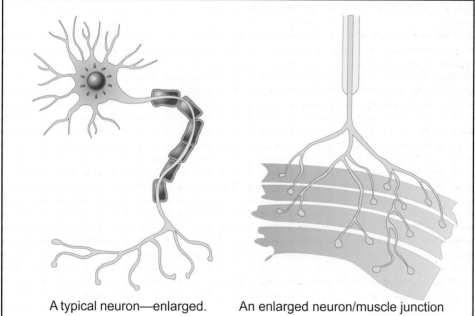

A typical neuron—enlarged.   An enlarged neuron/muscle junction

Where it all happens

B. Discriminative touch:

As an introduction to the somatosensory system, we will start by looking in some detail at the *discriminative* touch system. The system that is carried in the spinal cord includes the entire body from the neck down; face information is carried by cranial nerves; we will come back to it later.

Several types of mechanoreceptors are known, including free nerve endings.

The **pain and temperature** system does not have specialised receptor organs. Instead, it uses **free nerve endings** throughout skin, muscle, bone, and connective tissue to perceive changes in temperature and pain peptides. Although pain will result from damage to a free nerve ending, in reality most pain is a result of substances released by damaged tissues: **prostaglandins**, **histamine**, and **substance P**. The free nerve ending has receptors for these substances and lets you know (stridently) when tissue has been damaged.

The Oral Cavity—or the Mouth

The mouth is supplied by nerve endings from the 5th, 7th and 9th cranial nerves. These provide the receptors that subserve the senses of touch mentioned above. In addition, those cranial nerves carry the information from the taste buds

Following the sight and smell appraisals, the mouth becomes the wine evaluator's principal tool-of-trade. As mentioned on page 113, one of the 'hand-me-downs' from the past is the use of the revolting word 'palate'— 'he/she has a good palate'. My fascination is that the palate, particularly the hard palate, has little to do with our ability to perceive or discriminate the sense of taste or flavour. It is for this reason that, in this work, there are references to the oral cavity, starting with the lips, gums, teeth (rarely mentioned in references to perception), cheeks, tongue and throat. However, the roof of the mouth, the *hard* palate, has an important role in both the touch and mechanical senses.

As noted in the Smell chapter (page 51), during wine appraisal, a touch sense starts with the act of smelling when we are able to perceive high levels of SO_2 and alcohol as irritants. While it is thought that these vapours do stimulate the free nerve endings of the trigeminal nerves, they are perceived as irritants or pain rather than smell and, as such, can be understood as feel or touch sensations.

When I poll wine lovers around the world regarding the importance of the various senses used in food and beverage evaluation, touch is rarely mentioned; no city or nation has any monopoly in this area. Yet, after smell, touch must vie with colour as the next most important sense. Why then is touch more important than taste?

Erroneously, taste has historically been associated with touch and flavour, and only in recent times have these terms been rightfully separated. If we are to fully understand the true nature of our senses and the part they play in evaluation, we must be definitive about these terms and their roles.

As with colour, the importance of the tactile sense has never been stressed and I can only put this down to the fact that we know so little about the subject.

While the tactile sense is perceived mainly on the tongue by the *filiform* papillae, the hard palate, cheeks and gums are also a large area of perception.

Touch and mechanical senses

Why?

The filiform papillae are:

The most numerous tongue papillae and are pinkish grey in colour and tapering, threadlike points arranged in "V" shaped rows. They aid in food and beverage evaluation and contain touch sensory nerve endings.

The tactile sense gives us the mouth feel in food and beverages and covers our responses to the salient points of:

- **Temperature**—hot, warm, cold.
- **Pain and irritation**—burning, itching, pricking, aching, sharp pain.
- **Pressure: light touch**—as a mosquito on your nose; firm touch—as in sitting down.
- **Vibration**—gas, bubbles in wine, also rough and smooth.
- **Spatial**—form/shape. The *detection* of the *shape* of an *object*.

Temperature

Normal thermal sense is the ability to feel internal or external temperature. Basically, thermal sense tells you whether the ambient temperature or the temperature of an object is hot or cold, and approximately what that temperature is. Do not overlook this valuable part of wine evaluation.

It is thought that the mouth contains fewer warm-hot receptors than the fingers—one of the reasons why we can drink hot beverages that are too hot when spilt on other parts of our body. Even so, we are able to make judgments of slight temperature variation—and temperature is, possibly, the touch sense that is paramount in our evaluation of food and beverages.

Few people enjoy cola, beer or whisky, if they are served warm—or a roast dinner or hamburger that's cold. Despite the temperature difference, they really do *taste* the same even if the flavour is different. However, they are perceived quite differently, mainly because of the lack of smell stimulus. Or after being processed by the brain which has been programmed according to our cultural or family backgrounds. A cold beer tastes better to a thirsty person on a hot day. Is the satisfaction from the coldness, flavour, taste, or the brain's program? People can live without beer and receive similar pleasure from cold water, wine, tea or fruit juices. Many people enjoy hot tea, coffee or curry on hot days.

Coldness is a first-class anaesthetic. Why then do we have whisky and other spirits 'on the rocks', ice-cold cola or almost frozen beer? Is this done deliberately to kill the flavour? Such drastic temperature reduction can do nothing other than nullify the flavour and aroma of any food or beverage. Many years ago the chefs of the world realized the aroma benefits of serving hot food, so much so that nowadays we refuse food that is not piping hot, regardless of how good the flavour is. At the other extreme, beverages such as tea or coffee that are too hot are also tasteless.

Champagne is served cold 3.3°C (36–42°F) as coldness retains the bubbles in solution thus adding to the essential character of the beverage. As white wines and rosés have no bubbles there is no benefit (other than loss of flavour and

Do not overlook

Brain programming

125

aroma) in chilling them to the same low temperature. For these styles 10°C(50°F) is ideal. The only exception is a wine with undesirably high amounts of SO_2; the coldness will reduce the volatility of this unpleasant gas. Many faulty wines can be passed off in this manner.

Unfortunately, the international wine lover has been intimidated into believing that red wines should be served at 'room' temperature (without being told that this odd measurement of temperature approximates 18.3°C (65°F), and that white wines should be served at nearly freezing temperature. In warm climates I always ask for an ice bucket to cool my red wines. In cold climates I play a continual 'chess game' with wine waiters as I take near frozen bottles of white wine from the ice bucket, only to see waiters return and carefully snuggle the bottle back among the frozen chips.

During seminars in many countries I have introduced a pair of identical wines—one served chilled, the other warm. The warmer wine appears to be fuller bodied (more viscous) and sweeter while the colder wine is perceived as more acid and less viscous i.e. thinner/lighter. Also, the colder wine will be far less volatile and any bitterness will be less obvious.

This is important

A good example of this was quoted in the *Akron Beacon Journal* by Katherine Brewster after she attended one of my seminars in Cleveland, Ohio. 'Young even plays dirty tricks to hammer home the notion that wines are best evaluated when served at the proper temperatures. Participants are asked to judge two white wines. Discussion provokes vast differences in what turns out to be two identical wines served in extreme opposite temperature conditions.' Now, this seminar wasn't a group of new chums, rather a group of winemakers, importers and generally well informed people. How could this happen? Easily, and it does everyday to the unsuspecting and untrained.

Pain—Irritation

Webster's dictionary states that pain is 'the ability to sense a bodily disorder (as a disease or an injury) or a noxious stimulus, characterized by physical discomfort such as pricking, throbbing, or aching, and typically leading to evasive action.'

Pain sense also tells you what part of your body hurts, what type of hurt it is (throb, ache, sting, etc.), and how much it hurts.

Pain sense

Pain can take many forms other than the typical stabbing or throbbing pain. Hunger, need to excrete, fatigue, nausea, shortness of breath, and other symptoms are special effects of the pain sense telling the brain that there is something wrong with the body.

The pain and temperature senses use *free nerve endings* throughout the skin, muscle, bone and connective tissues to perceive changes in temperature and pain peptides (any of various natural or synthetic compounds containing two or more amino acids.)

These are important factors in our food and beverage assessment. Indians love hot curries, far hotter than the capacity of most Caucasians. Hot chillies are enjoyed throughout the Spanish speaking world and the cultures of the Far East. Only in recent times (1985) has the 'hot' component of chili been identified as capsaicin. This also brought into prominence another sensory system, the poly-monol-nocice, which responds to both chemical and hot temperature stimulation.

There is a Richter-type scale, known as Scoville units, for measuring the heat units of capsaicin in various peppers graduating from zero in the ordinary capsicums (bell peppers) to Habaneros—the hottest of all peppers -register a blistering 200,000 to 300,000 units. The common jalopino pepper which many people think are very hot are, in fact, almost at the bottom of the heat range with 2.5–3.5K units. Pure capsaicin has a Scoville heat unit score of 16 million. Other scores include cayenne peppers at 30–50K while the Thai peppers run between 50–100K.

Pepper steaks and black pepper dishes are increasingly popular in the western cuisine; obviously an acceptable level of irritation from peppers, curry, mustard and other spices can be pleasant flavour sensations. Or, are they as discussed under *texture*, the enjoyment of a new textural feeling as introduced by the large pepper grains?

The pepper character (as opposed to the hot/peppery sensation of high alcohol wine) can be perceived in both the smell and 'mouth feel' of particular red wines, notably Zinfandel and Syrah from cool growing regions.

Pain and irritation sensations in beverages are generated by a number of wine components:

- Alcohol—above 12 per cent by volume, ethanol impinges on the pain receptors in the bottom of the nasal cavity. Higher levels of alcohol in wine can also irritate the eyes.

- Sulphur dioxide (SO_2) is the one component used from the time the grapes are picked until the finished wine is bottled. In correct proportions (20–100 ppm—parts per million) with the exception of the sweet white Sauternes styles where the amount ranges 150–200 ppm), SO_2 is an important stabilizing agent used for anti-bacterial purposes and as an oxidant inhibitor. Above 175 ppm SO_2 becomes a negative factor evidenced by a burnt match smell that impinges on the free nerve endings inside the top of the nose during the smell appraisal, plus leaving a drying condition in the mouth (particularly during the after-flavour that is most noticeable on the roof of the mouth.

SO_2 is expressed as *bound, free* and *total* sulphur. Bound sulphur is that chemically bound to compounds such as the carbonyls which include acetaldehyde. SO_2 also binds to sugars. Free sulphur, as the name suggests, is unbound and able to be volatilised (freed from the wine).

Surprisingly, total sulphur (unlike acids) is the combination of bound and free sulphur.

If you have a wine exhibiting excessive sulphur, try pouring it from one container to another—back and forth several times—the more splashing the better. This will allow the gas to escape and the wine will be far more pleasant, if ever so slightly oxidized. Just simply allowing the wine to sit in the glass or carafe will help the sulphur volatilise.

Hot chillies

Sulphur dioxide

127

Pressure

This is the form—the shape and weight-of the food or beverage in the mouth. The main components affecting pressure in wine are:

- Grape tannin.
- Wood tannin.
- Viscosity—a combination of sugar, alcohol and the polymers—tannins and pro-anthocyanins.

Fortified wines containing higher alcohol and particularly those with sugar, exert more pressure on the nerve endings and give us the feeling of viscosity. The contributing components of viscosity/body are: sugar discussed in the taste chapter; alcohol—discussed below; glycerol—a colourless, odourless, viscous liquid which is very sweet and obtained as a by product of grape sugar fermentation. (Also used in the manufacture of explosives, cellulose films, synthetic resins and many other products.)

Vibration—Gas—Carbon Dioxide (CO_2) in Wine

Most people are familiar with the importance of the CO_2 component in sparkling wines (it gives them the sparkle.) Gas can be noticed in many white wines, and, indeed some red wines, both by design and by unfavourable accident. The bubbles that appear in white table wines and can be seen adhering to the bottom insides of the glass are known as *'spritzig'* (German) or French *'petillant'*. They are a product of bottling procedures—gas being absorbed into the wine at cold temperatures, indicate that the wine has been carefully handled at that time, but in no way reflects the quality of the wine.

Texture

While much of the following refers to food, it applies equally to beverages.

Food scientists and researchers

Food scientists and researchers have wrestled with the definition of just the texture part of the tactile sense for many years and still agree to disagree. As of 2008, there is no single definition of texture, which plays a major role in the evaluation of both food and beverages. Jowett (1974) offers this definition of texture: 'The attribute of a substance resulting from a combination of physical properties and perceived by the senses of touch (including kinesthesis and mouth feel), sight and hearing. Physical properties may include size, shape, number, nature and conformation of constituent structural elements.'

Yet, here are three more definitions: 'the manner of structure, interrelation of parts, structural quality.'

Texture (*noun*): All the mechanical (geometrical and surface) attributes of a food product perceptible by means of mechanical, tactile and, where appropriate, visual and auditory receptors (International Organization for Standardization, Standard 5492, 1992).

Texture is the human physiological-psychological perception of the attributes resulting from a combination of physical properties perceived by the senses of kinesthesis, touch (including mouth, feel, sight and hearing). The properties may include size, shape, number, nature, and conformation of constituent structural elements. (British Standards Organization No. 5098).

Texture is a group of physical properties that derive from the structure of food or beverages. It is not related to the chemical senses of taste or odour.

A major challenge facing food developers is how to accurately and objectively measure texture and mouth feel. Texture is a composite property related to a number of physical properties (e.g., viscosity and elasticity), and the relationship is complex. Describing texture or mouth feel in a single value obtained from an instrument is impossible. Mouth feel is difficult to define. It involves food and beverages entire physical and chemical interactions in the mouth—from initial perception in the mouth, to first sip, through the act of swallowing.

Texture and mouth feel

General Foods' Texture Profile Analysis (TPA) technique forms the basis of most standard methods of mouth feel analysis used today. A.S. Szczesniak proposed a classification of food texture based on rheological principles which could be monitored by both instrumental and sensory methods of texture characterization. She classified the textural characteristics of food into mechanical, geometrical and 'other' properties. The mechanical properties were subdivided into five primary parameters (hardness, cohesiveness, viscosity, elasticity and adhesiveness) and three secondary parameters (brittleness, chewiness and gumminess). The geometrical characteristics were divided into two general groups—those related to size and shape of particles and those related to shape and orientation. This applies equally to wine.

Flavour, comprising taste (perceived in the mouth) and odour (perceived in the olfactory center above the nose), is the response of receptors in the oral and nasal cavities to chemical stimuli. These are called 'the chemical senses'.

Texture is primarily the response of the tactile senses to physical stimuli that result from contact between some part of the body and the food. The tactile sense (touch) is the primary method for sensing texture but kinesthetics (sense of movement and position) and sometimes sight (degree of slump, rate of flow), and sound (associated with crisp, crunchy and crackly textures) are also used to evaluate texture.

Physical stimuli

The importance of texture in the overall acceptability of foods varies widely, depending upon the type of food. We could arbitrarily break it into three groups:

- **Critical:** Foods in which texture is the dominant quality characteristic; for example, meat, potato chips, corn flakes, apples and celery.

- **Important:** Foods in which texture makes a significant but not a dominant contribution to the overall quality, contributing, more or less equally, with flavor and appearance. Most fruits, vegetables, cheeses, bread, most other cereal-based foods fall into this category.

- **Minor:** Foods in which texture makes a negligible contribution to the overall quality. Examples are most beverages and thin soups.

Young adults of normal weight were able to identify correctly only 41% of the foods used in a recent study. It could be surprising to find that only 4% of the respondents could identify cabbage correctly by flavour only, 15% for pork, 41% for beef, and 51% for carrots.

The importance of texture, relative to other quality factors of foods is affected by culture. For example, in a study of food patterns of the United States and Caribbean-African culture people, Jerome (1975) stated: 'For Afro-Americans of southern rural origin, the element of primary importance associated with food patterns is *texture*; flavour assumes secondary importance.'

These authors concluded that texture is a discernible characteristic, but that it is more evident in some foods than others. Foods that elicited the highest number of texture responses either were bland in flavour or possessed the characteristics of crunchiness or crispness.

Time of day

Szczesniak and Kahn (1971) reported that *time of day* exerted a strong influence on textural awareness and flavour. At breakfast, most people prefer a restricted range of familiar textures that lubricate the mouth, remove the dryness of sleep, and can be swallowed without difficulty.

New or unfamiliar textures, and textures that are difficult to chew, may not be wanted at breakfast. People are willing to accept a wider range of textures at the midday meal just so long as it is quick and easy to prepare and not messy to eat. After all, this is a practical meal with a limited time for preparation and consumption.

The Universal TA-XT2 Texture Analyzer (from Texture Technologies Corp., Scarsdale, NY), which can perform a complete Texture Profiling Analysis calculation, comes with 25 standard probes, including various sizes of needles, cones, cylinders, punches, knives and balls. It can determine adhesion, bloom strength, breaking point, cohesion, creep, crispiness, density, extrudability, film strength, hardness, lumpiness, rubberiness, slipperiness, smoothness, softness, spreadability, springback, tackiness, tensile strength and nearly every other known rheological property of foods.

Digital equipment

To me, this does mean that wine quality evaluation will soon move to digital equipment rather than the manner it is performed by humans—organoleptic assessment, and the term will go.

Definitions—Texture terms used in sensory texture profiling

Anthocyanins: Any of various water-soluble pigments that impart to flowers and other plant parts colours ranging from violet and blue to most shades of red. Colouring matter in red wines.

Coarseness: Degree to which the mass feels coarse during the evaluation.

Dryness: Degree to which the wine gives a drying feeling in the mouth.

Graininess: Degree to which a sample contains small grainy particles.

Heaviness: Weight of wine perceived when first placed on tongue.

Mouthcoating: Type and degree of coating in the mouth.

Mucins: Any of a group of glycoproteins (non-carbohydrates) found especially in the secretions of mucous membranes.

Organoleptic: Involving the use of sense organs: *organoleptic tests*. This term was widely used by the wine industry some two decades ago but is still in use in the food industry.

Polymerise: To cause polymerization of; to produce polymers from; to increase the molecular weight of, without changing the atomic proportions; thus, certain acids polymerize aldehyde.

Rheological: The study of the deformation and flow of matter.

Roughness: Degree of abrasiveness of wines surface perceived in the mouth.

Smoothness: Absence of any particles, lumps, bumps, etc., e.g. increased sugar levels.

Synapses: The junction across which a nerve impulse passes from an axon terminal to a neuron, muscle cell, from Greek sunapsis, *point of contact*.

Uniformity: Degree to which the sample is even throughout—as opposed to balance where all components are well-balanced.

Viscosity: resistance of a liquid to sheer forces (and hence to flow)—we can now use a viscometer to measure viscosity

Alcohol

The main alcohol resulting from the fermentation of the grape sugars, fructose and glucose, is ethyl alcohol (ethanol). Other alcohols with longer carbon chains exist in small amounts and play an important role in the aroma, flavour and general form of the wine. Ethanol gives wine body or viscosity. Table wines with low ethanol content have a 'thin' (low viscosity) character and those with too high concentrations can be flat and 'hot'. (If the lady's orange or tomato juice has a hot spot in the middle of the tongue beware! Someone has added a healthy slug of alcohol.)

Like any other anaesthesia, the first action of ethyl alcohol is on the highest centers of the brain, with emotions, inhibitions, judgment and mental clarity being affected. Further amounts increasingly affect the central nervous system, decreasing muscular coordination, perception and reaction time. This is the basic problem with drinking alcohol and driving a vehicle.

First action of alcohol

Alcohol can irritate the eyes to the extent that when smelling some high alcohol wines your eyes will actually weep. Alcohol normally registers as warmth in the center of the tongue. High alcohol wines are 'hot' (and maybe peppery) all over the mouth, causing pain or irritation and leaving a 'drying' sensation. This hot sensation can be greatly increased by the combination of ethanol and the bitter substance quinine sulphate.

Alcohol Levels

The 21st century gave us fermentation yeasts that extract almost every gram of sugar and normal alcohol levels have increased. Some indications of what you may now see in popular wine styles are:

White, rosé and red table wines: 10–15 per cent by volume, some German white table wines as little as 7 per cent; some New World red and white table wines are higher in alcohol reaching up to 16%. Sherry, Port, vermouth, marsala and flavoured wines: 17–21%.

The aroma, touch and taste perception of alcohol, more particularly in the fortified wines, depends largely on the wine style. Wines containing high sugar levels (such as port and the sweeter sherry styles) tend to have even the harshest alcohol masked; while styles such as the drier sherries, say fino, without the sugar mask, but with high levels of both alcohol and aldehydes, can, at times, exhibit the pain sense.

Alcohol Exercise

Make up an alcohol water solution by adding a dessert spoon of vodka to three ounces of water. Note the smoothness and fullness of body/viscosity plus the warm spot on the tongue- this will probably be accompanied by a persistent irritation or overall warmth in the mouth during the aftertaste. If more than 12 per cent by volume when smelt, you will notice irritation in the lower part of the nose; sometimes this takes a minute or so to register.

If you receive no response from the alcohol and water mix, keep adding vodka by half teaspoon measures until you are able to perceive the irritation and heat sensations. Note the contributions to viscosity and sweetness.

Alcohol Record Chart

Record your perception of these components on a scale of 10

		Weak 1 2 3	Moderate 4 5 6 7	Strong 8 9 10
Teeth	Upper	. . .	. . . .	. . .
	Lower	. . .	. . . .	. . .
Gums	Upper	. . .	. . . .	. . .
	Lower	. . .	. . . .	. . .
Lips	Upper	. . .	. . . .	. . .
	Lower	. . .	. . . .	. . .
Tongue	Tip	. . .	. . . .	. . .
	Top	. . .	. . . .	. . .
	Sides	. . .	. . . .	. . .
Cheeks	Front	. . .	. . . .	. . .
	Rear	. . .	. . . .	. . .
Throat		. . .	. . . .	. . .
Roof of mouth				

Alcohol Words

Negative (too little)	Positive	Negative (too much)
Thin	Warm	Coarse
Watery	Round	Hot
	Balanced	Drying

Next time you're near the brandy bottle, pour a shot into a glass, swirl it around and take a sniff. It will most probably go close to lifting off your head, because of the almost 80 per cent proof alcohol (40 per cent by vol). Now, dilute this with an equal amount of water and take another sniff -you should be able to pick up all sorts of nuances because you're not being assaulted by the spirit. Maybe there is a sniff of the original wine, maybe the vanillin of oak. Brandy has a complexity of flavours and aromas if you can quell the alcohol. Of course, these subtleties are all lost when we have spirits 'on the rocks'.

One problem in evaluating a number of high alcohol wines can be that the alcohol enters the bloodstream through the oral cavity mucous membranes. Yes, you can get 'high' without swallowing a drop.

TANNINS

Grape tannins that are responsible for the sense of touch are polymeric flavan-3 ols and are called *proanthocyanins* or condensed tannins and they are mainly esterified to gallic acid.

They create astringent and bitter mouth sensations with bitterness perceived just *before* astringency. Astringency is due to the interaction of these compounds with saliva, reducing the lubrication of saliva. This varies with individuals as well as the concentration and polymerisation and wine pH.

Bitterness and astringency

The various saliva glands in different regions of the mouth produce different mucins (discharges), under the tongue, back of the mouth and on the cheeks. These are similar but different, to those around the gums and the floor of the mouth. Oak tannins tend to be highly polymerised with large molecular weights such as castaline and corilagin but the degree of toasting during coopering and the source of the oak, European or American, influence this.

Nevertheless the tactile perception of the oak tannins is mainly on the cheeks because of this composition. As mentioned in the bitterness section, bitterness and astringency go hand-in-hand, bitter being a true *taste* sensation, while astringency stimulates the touch sense.

Although we don't have high tolerances for bitterness or astringency, most of our popular beverages are moderately high in phenolic substances, the providers for both sensations. Here's a run down on the polyphenols in these favoured beverages: coffee heads the list with 2000 parts per million (ppm), tea next with 1600 ppm, red wine has 1300 ppm, European beer and American beer about half the European figure. Vanilla, cinnamon and spicy substances are some of the other flavour benefits originating from grape phenolics. But, as tannins provide much of wine's sensory character, we will deal with that here. As mentioned in the colour chapter, wine's colour pigments are also phenolic substances—anthocyanins.

Wine has both grape and wood tannins, both with similar touch sensations; my experience is that we perceive them in different parts of the mouth. Grape tannin is more likely to be noticeable on the teeth, lips and front of the cheeks as a rough, 'furry' sensation; wood tannin is more of a warm sensation on the insides of the cheeks, further to the rear.

Grape and oak tannins

Grape tannin is bitter and high levels can cause mild pain by acting on the free nerve endings. 'Grip' is a word associated with the mouth feel of grape tannin, particularly when the gripping sensation can be so assertive that you think that your teeth are being drawn out through your ears!

Grape tannin is often called the 'backbone' or 'spine' of the wine. Grapes from warm-hot regions have less natural tannin and colour than wines from cold or cool regions, not that this is a disadvantage if the wine is to be sold as a 'drink now' style. It is also quite legal in the New World to add tannin as it is a natural grape product. Added tannin also aids in colour stability. Can great wines be made in a warm-hot regions? Very definitely yes; in fact, these areas are my preference for wines other than Pinot noir.

Provided that highly tannic wines are combined with a commensurate amount of fruit and acid, they have the potential for a long cellaring life. It can be assumed that a higher degree of grape tannin is a measure of the wine's ability to age gracefully; for what that is worth?

In young wines, this tannin can be unattractive; it is best that we don't always rush our reds. Your trusted wine merchant, not just any chain store, can provide you with advice and examples here.

Astringency Exercises

To learn more about the mouth feel of astringency, go to your local pharmacist or florist and obtain a pinch of alum. Add this to an ounce of water and roll this mix around your mouth. If you do this, you have my guarantee that you will not quickly forget what astringency is, and, forever you will be able to differentiate between astringency and bitterness.

Astringency exercise

For the tannin mix, you will need to obtain a little grape tannin from your local home winemaker supply store, most sell either chips or granules about the size of sugar. Mix these with a little vodka or ethanol and add to wine rather than water. Tannin is not easy to mix with water, the vodka helps in this regard A large pinch should be sufficient for a two person wine sample, preferably red. Have something pleasant to rinse your mouth or drink after doing both these mixes—they are not likely to be among your great flavour sensations; but certainly a great learning experience.

Procedure for mixing tannin and oak chips.

Tannin exercise

This exercise, as most others, is best done with a small group as it is just as easy to set-it-up for four-six people as it is for one person. Select a regular jug or cask red, preferably one that has not had any obvious oak.

Have ready four empty 300ml plastic water bottles marked: Control, tannin, oak #1 and oak #2. Fill bottles with wine, less one tablespoon. Screw cap on

Two University Home Training Kits are available from The International Wine Academy—one, the UWTK which deals solely with sensory evaluation and is a companion to this book. The other kit, Home Study—Level One combines sensory evaluation, viticulture and wine production. Both kits include the necessary wine components (except vodka and sugar) to complete the exercises in the Taste and Touch chapters. The components include: acid, tannin, a source of SO_2, oak chips, and alum.

control bottle. Add one eighth of a teaspoon of tannin which has been mixed with a teaspoon of vodka into *tannin* bottle and screw-on lid.

Add one level tablespoon of no-toast or light-toast chips to bottle #3 (oak #1) and screw-on lid. Repeat with oak #2 in bottle #4. Leave the two oaked bottles on their sides and rotate daily for 4–6 days.

On the judging day, you are judging or evaluating these wines, not *tasting*!

Each person should have four glasses with a 30–40ml (1-1½ ounces) sample of each component in the four glasses, working from the left which has the control wine. After tasting wines 2–4, go back to the control wine each time before proceeding with the next sample.

Work with your component record sheets for tannin and oak and record your perceptions of these various components. Where in the mouth do they register strongest? Then score the wines on the WER score sheet.

When you have completed these exercises, assuming that you have an equal amount in each glass, mix all glasses together and score this wine as wine #5; you will be amazed at what you have done.

Tannin Record Chart

Record your perception of this component with an X on a scale of 10

		Week 1 2 3	Moderate 4 5 6 7	Strong 8 9 10
Teeth	Upper	. . .	. . . .	. . .
	Lower	. . .	. . . .	. . .
Gum	Upper	. . .	. . . .	. . .
	Lower	. . .	. . . .	. . .
Lips	Upper	. . .	. . . .	. . .
	Lower		. . . .	. . . .
Tongue	Tip	. . .	. . . .	. . .
	Top	. . .	. . . .	. . .
	Sides	. . .	. . . .	. . .
	Rear	. . .	. . . .	. . .
Throat		. . .	. . . .	. . .
Roof of mouth		. . .	. . . .	. . .

STRUCTURE

Before explaining structure it would be best to explain, in another way, why this is an important subject. Australian winemaker and longtime wine judge, Viv Thomson, has described wines as being either *talking* or *drinking* wines. The wines we talk about are the higher priced wines that are kept for special occasions—and the drinking wines are those we have with our daily meals.

'Drinking' &
'talking' wines

Drinking wines are becoming better each year and most represent excellent value. Talking wines are the ones that are the subject of discussion about *structure*. Unfortunately, over the years, a lot of myths have grown-up surrounded by mystical wine twaddle. Regrettably, the wines of France's Bordeaux and Burgundy regions have been used as a quality benchmark as they were the desired wines mostly available at good wine stores and restaurants. The French have certainly done wonders in entering the minds of people throughout the world with a false message.

Forty years ago and before, it was a poor restaurant or wine store that did not have at least three vintages of the favoured Bordeaux or Burgundy labels—and these wines were at least 10, if not 15–20, years of age. Of course, those days are gone with the mad rush to move wines from the cellar to the consumer. Today, most consumers have, sadly, never enjoyed a wine that has reached its peak of drinkability.

This brought about the incredible notion that *all* wine had to be capable of long-cellaring to be any good. In fact, that was the truth because these benchmark, expensive wines were so badly made that long cellaring was necessary to overcome the excessive tannin problem inherent in them. There was also the hope that people would eventually become anxious to drink these ageing monsters before they went over the distant hill.

Impossibility

Today, it would be impossible give away, let alone sell at totally ridiculous prices, wines of that quality and style. It should be said that the *top* (Grand crus) Bordeaux and Burgundy wines represent a mere three percent of all wines made in those districts. It is true that I am not a buyer of these wines, nor do I think that the average reader of this book will be in the $200–900 per bottle drinking category. At the time of going to publication it is impossible to put more than US$20 into a bottle of the best wine, consistent with the producer being the winery and equipment owner. So where do these crazy prices emanate?

That figure is arrived at on the premise that the very best grapes, new barrels, bottles, corks, labels and cartons are used and allowing for the contract price for making and bottling wine. It is beyond the scope of this book to completely analyse every cost such as borrowed money and fallacious promotional costs.

Sadly we have been left with this long-cellaring legacy, and a wine's ability to cellar for a long time is still a criterion demanded by many. Most wine lovers believe that wine is made to drink and enjoy—and not be auctioned or traded like junk bonds, washing machines or all the useless articles in your garage.

This preamble is necessary to explain the reason to understand wine structure which is important when discussing *drinking* wines. Wine structure is a hard word to define—but is a decisive word in wine communication and evaluation. Eminent French educator, Professor Emile Peynaud, describes structure as, *'also impressions of **volume, form** and **consistency**. He (the taster) forms a **physical image of the wine.**'*

Definition

At an international wine conference in New Zealand, I asked one winemaker from each of four continents to define the word *structure* and received a mixed bag of definitions. After taking into account the culture and the language of four continents, the consensus was:

- How the wine is built.
- All wines have a beginning, middle and an end, in varying degrees.
- The feeling of the tannin, acid and alcohol—and how the wine holds together.
- Concentration of flavour, body and strength.

Reviewing this potpourri of opinions, the paramount phrase seems to be *how the wine is built*; the other utterances supporting this simple phrase.

Elements of structure

Although very important in flavour, structure does not relate to smell or taste but, rather, touch; *how the wine is built*. However, *oak* treatment, or the lack of it, does play an important part in structure. During your previous exercises with red wine, tannin and oak in this chapter, you will have noticed an important difference in each of these wines; those are simply a *flavour* and *structural* difference. The various oak amounts and the tannin addition changed the flavour and structure of all but the control wine. At the end of the exercise, you obviously observed that the control wine was a hopeless wimp.

Important differences

Glycerol or *glycerine* is a by-product of fermentation and a natural product in wine that is important to mouth feel, texture and structure. Glycerol has the texture of light oil or a syrupy, sugar-water solution, thereby contributing generously to structure, texture and mouth feel

Diacetyl is the love/hate by-product of malolactic fermentation. At levels below 1.5 ppm it plays out its love role in subduing phenolic and related bitterness in red wines, and in some of the 'bigger' Chardonnays. It does this by smoothing the mouth feel, thus lightening the effect on pressure receptors and relieving the astringency feeling. Diacetyl is identified by its 'buttery' smell—in fact, diacetyl is added to margarine to make it smell like butter. In everyday use, diacetyl is found in cheese, adding that buttery smell, especially to cheddars. In beer it also provides a buttery smell, but it can also contribute to sourness.

Diacetyl

The other main parts of structure: alcohol and tannin have been discussed on pages 129–133.

Drinkability

Of all the important considerations about wine, none is more important than drinkability. This is a very personal choice as Paul Rigby gleefully illustrates at the beginning of chapter 1.

What is drinkability—how pretty is that girl? Think about it, you may know what drinkability is, but can you explain it to yourself and others? Obviously it means that the wine must be drinkable, yet, as explained many times in this work, perception is very much a personal thing.

Viticultural understanding

One of the reasons to study the basics of viticulture is to have a better understanding of what makes wine what it is. The largest percentage of the world's wine comes from the mostly irrigated, large desert regions of the world, more particularly those from Australia, Argentina, California and South Africa.

The Languedoc-Roussillon and other southern regions of France, La Mancha in Spain and Sicily can be classified neither as desert nor irrigated, yet they produce enormous amounts of wine, both good and poor. France's almost unknown southern regions produce about 40 percent of that country's wine. It is inevitable that irrigation will eventually come to these regions.

These wines, either red or white, are, mainly, drinkable at an early age whereas wines from colder regions require a longer period of bottle and/or barrel age to reach drinkability.

So, some wines are eminently drinkable at one to two years of age while others require evolution (or maturation) of three to more than 10 years to reach drinkability.

How then does one explain drinkability? Possibly a crude definition is one that the wine has no 'rough edges,' has no glaring amounts of alcohol, acid, oak or tannins yet has good amounts of fruit and evolution, i.e. the wine has 'come together'—now.

Another view

Noted New Zealand author and writer, Peter Saunders, has this to say:

'There are so many wine descriptors which are non-specific. In a scientific way, who can say what is elegant, classy, high/low drinkability factor, lovely, floral or delicious?'

We know and have proven from tastings that one woman's passionfruit is another man's oyster. And tannic today can be rounded-off in two years, or two months in a warm cellar.

But the inference of elegant, aromatic or delicious is specific to that tasting note by that person on that day with that bottle of wine. But the inference is perfectly clear. *Implicit rather than explicit.*

Accessability

So I take 'drinkability factor' to rate accessibility as of today, presumably lower tannins, higher pH, balanced of course, fruit expansive, generous, not wood dominated as of now, nor any other extra or preservative but—ready and enjoyable wine to the person making the comment.

"The implicity of drinkability is that I can drink it now with enjoyment."

FEEL WHEEL

Scientists at the Australian Wine Research Institute have done some exploratory work on the *touch wheel* modelled on the Aroma Wheel. I think a lot more work needs to be done on it as this is the key to higher learning in the practise of sensory evaluation.

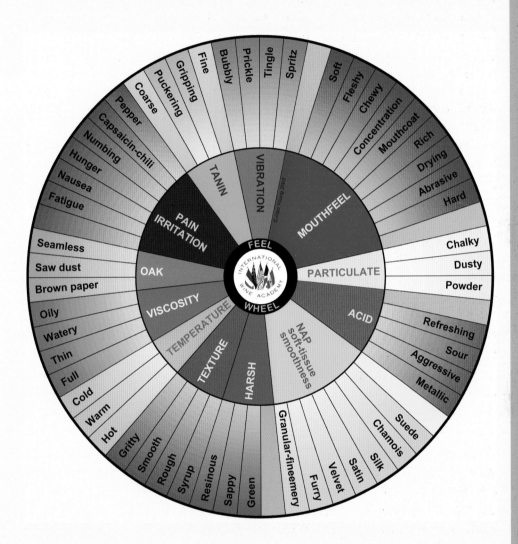

1. Mouth feel involves the entire physical and chemical interactions of food and beverages in the mouth — from initial perception in the mouth, to first sip, right through the act of swallowing.

2. Mouth feel does not include the chemical senses of smell and taste.

While it may sound strange, wine is described in many shapes: round, angular, big, fat, thin, etc..

Barriques being filled beside cold-jacketed stainless steel tanks
in a California winery.

Barriques in new "Meccano" type stack in a Spanish winery.

OAK IN WINE—WINE IN OAK

Let us start with the realistic definition that wine is *the wholly or partially fermented juice of grapes*. Nothing here about oak—and this should always be remembered when talking about or defining wine. Wine is the fermented juice of grapes. Anything that is not from the grape is now, and has been for 8,000 years, foreign to wine.

For these many millennia, the world lived without the taste of burnt wood. Be very wary of what oak in wine truly is. You will see and hear about many wines that have been made in heavily toasted barrels. In many cases, this wine has never been in contact with the oak; rather it has been in contact with charcoal on the insides of the staves caused by excessive heating (firing) during the coopering stages, and this alligator skin appearance of charcoal is a very different substance to oak wood flavour. I am not making a case for either; I just want the wine lover to be discerning about what goes into their mouth.

Suitable white oak trees grow in many countries throughout Europe: Austria, Czech, France, Hungary, Poland, Russia, Slovenia plus others—and in North America including small stands in Mexico, a new (2002) supply emerging from quite large forests in Canada. Many eastern and northern US states are traditional suppliers of white oak, while Oregon oak has become available in the last decade.

Oak sources

There is much speculation about which oak is best. However, that comes down to personal choice, as some oaks are considered better for one wine style while another oak suits a different wine style. One classic answer to this dubious question came from longtime cooper, Ohio's William J. Weil. 'Firstly, we would have to build a consensus of what is best. Of all the opinions I have heard as to which is the best oak, without exception, they have been based upon either ignorance, emotion or self-promotion.'

The vast difference between the two main European and American white oaks is that the American *Quercas alba* can be sawn into barrel staves whereas the European oaks logs from *Quercas sessilflora* and *Quercas robur* must use the wasteful method of splitting the logs into four sections. American oak is rich in tyloses that plugs the tubes in the oak and makes this oak suitable as a container for liquids such as whisky, brandy, beer—and wine without the inherent waste.

Q. robur is often called English, French or Russian oak which, in days past, was used to build the ships for those once mighty navies. Oak is classified as fine or coarse grained which denotes the spacing difference in the spring to summer growth rings of the tree. Much of this is a reflection of the region and climate in which the trees grow—just as in grape vines—the trees reflect the amount of rainfall and sunshine—or *terroir* of that region.

Spacing differences

There is good and bad oak in all forests and the wine business uses only about three percent of available oak. The remainder goes to the building, furniture and veneer industries.

Red wines, and some white wines, can be improved, in both structure and flavour, by being placed in barrels, casks or vats—normally made of white oak. However, for centuries chestnut and beech barrels have been used in Portugal to make some of the world's finest Port style wines.

Like the wheel, the barrel is an amazing representation of the old fashioned BC technology. Even in the 21st century, with all the computer wizardry and high technology, nobody has been able to improve on the size, shape, structure or flavour of the oak barrel.

Originally the barrel was made for the *storage* and *transportation* of wine. Later a vertical open-top cask was developed for fermentation purposes and became popular throughout Europe.

Even later, through the genius of Louis Pasteur, we became familiar with the fermentation process and that enabled more scientific studies regarding the evolution (maturation) of wine in wooden casks.

What is a barrel?

While not popular in New World countries where there is a penchant for the small 225 to 230 litre *barriques*, many European wineries use larger barrels of 300 or 600 litres plus casks and vats of even greater capacity, each having a name in their own language. (See next page). Technically, a *barrel* contains 44 Imperial gallons or 200 litres, the measure used in the oil industry

Pasteur, and his successors' studies taught us that wine time in oak casks helped *stabilise* the colour of red wine. The small amounts of oxygen that came through the wood also provided the catalyst for a number of evolutionary chemical changes that benefited and softened the wine.

Well, that was in the days before 1950 when the wine world went mad and placed young wine in 100% new barrels. The next 50 years saw all sorts of experiments with new oak barrels and the patient wine lover was assaulted with some shocking unscientific experiments from people who had no idea of the definition of wine—or even considered the grape aspect. The thinking was that if a little oak was good, then a lot must be a whole lot better.

Without a doubt, excessive oak is *definitely* a fault in wine. Yet, our experiments at UWS in determining how much oak is too much have been confusing, to say the very least. See the table below.

HOW MUCH OAK IS TOO MUCH?

Treatment	Judge 1	2	3	4	5	6	7	8		
No oak	12	11	15	10.5	11.5	10	10	9	=	89
5 gms	15	11.3	17	13.3	13	9.5	11	10	=	101.1
10 gms	16.5	11.5	14	13	12.5	11	13	6	=	97.5
15 gms	13.8	8.7	14.5	15	12.5	9.5	14	9	=	97
20 gms	13.3	12.9	14	12	12	10	14	9	=	97.2
	=70.6	=55.4	=74.5	=63.8	=61.5	=50	=62	=43		

ANOVA : Single factor

Opposite: Large new, upright oak vats at a Spanish bodega.

This experiment was to determine the perception of different amounts of oak in wine—zero in the control wine, then 5, 10, 15, and 20 grams of medium toasted oak per litre were prepared in a good cask (bag-in-a-box) red.

The average judgements out of 20 points were 11.5 for the control wine (no oak), 13 points for the 5gms per litre added oak chips, 12.5 points for 10gms, 12.5 points for 15gms and 12points for the 20gms added oak chips. This would indicate that *this* group preferred slightly less oak.

The high cost of new barrels led to the introduction of oak chips to give wine the supposedly desired oaky flavour. More than 50% of American and 80% of European oak is wasted during the barrel making process and oak chips are a good source of recovering some of this huge wastage. In France, 80% of a grand old 150 years oak tree can be wasted.

Oak chips are available in a variety of styles including French and American oak. Three toast levels: light, medium and heavy plus untoasted. Oak also comes as a powder, sawdust and splinter type texture.

In addition to the above, oak flavour is obtainable as a liquid which is used mainly by amateur winemakers.

Micro-oxygenation

Micro-oxygenation of wine refers to the addition of only 10 to 100 parts per million of oxygen or air directly into wine and can be done at any stage of wine production. It brings about desirable increases in aroma, texture and colour. There is a reduction in undesirable mercaptan *q.v.*, and vegetative flavours, and the colour of red wine is stabilised.

Goldfish

If you have ever owned, or seen, a goldfish tank you will have observed the gentle trickle of oxygen bubbles coming out of a pipe in the tank. Remove the pipe from the tank—or increase the amount of oxygen flow—and the fish will soon die. That is micro-oxygenation in action to keep the fish in an environment in which they can live happily.

This is a similar natural action of a wooden wine barrel as opposed to an inert stainless steel, fibreglass or concrete wine tank. The wood allows this micro amount of oxygen into the wine without the cask leaking. This oxygen provides the catalyst for many favourable changes in the evolution or maturation of fine wine.

While a limited amount of wine judges may be able to identify wine aged in wooden casks, the average wine drinker doesn't understand the seamless nature of the difference between wine from casks—and oak chips added to wine in an inert tank. And, the day is not far away when the intricacies of micro-oxygenation will be mastered and the oak barrel will be just a showpiece—as are many other things connected with wine production.

It is preferable that most table wines are made in a manner that protects the young wine from oxidation or too much oxygen. You have seen it many times when you cut an apple or a pear and the cut surface soon goes brown; that is oxidation and is detrimental to good wine. Oak vessels (or cooperage) naturally ensures that wine does not oxidise—unless the bung is left-off the barrel or there is too much ullage (empty space between wine and top of barrel).

Entry of oxygen

Air can enter the wine during racking or through barrel staves but new micro-oxygenation machines have been developed that continually feed oxygen into the wine. This oxygen is absorbed within hours.

The mechanism whereby oxygen benefits colour and flavour is by interacting with anthocyanin and flavanoid pigments and removing astringent phenolic compounds. Oxygenation must be controlled because excessive use may polymerise tannins resulting in turbidity in the wine.

Commercial micro-oxygenation units have been on the market since 1996, with more than 1700 units being used in wineries world wide as of 2004.

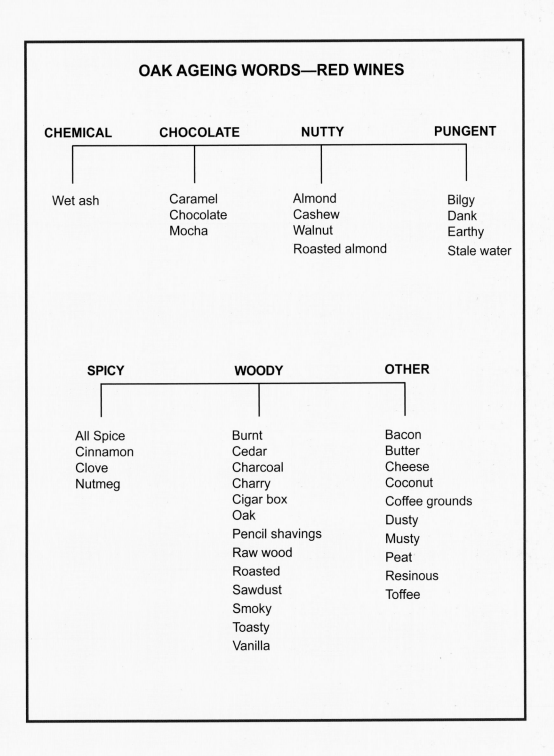

OAK AGEING WORDS—RED WINES

CHEMICAL	CHOCOLATE	NUTTY	PUNGENT
Wet ash	Caramel	Almond	Bilgy
	Chocolate	Cashew	Dank
	Mocha	Walnut	Earthy
		Roasted almond	Stale water

SPICY	WOODY	OTHER
All Spice	Burnt	Bacon
Cinnamon	Cedar	Butter
Clove	Charcoal	Cheese
Nutmeg	Charry	Coconut
	Cigar box	Coffee grounds
	Oak	Dusty
	Pencil shavings	Musty
	Raw wood	Peat
	Roasted	Resinous
	Sawdust	Toffee
	Smoky	
	Toasty	
	Vanilla	

A TOUCHING SUMMARY

- The touch sense, in all its forms, is the least understood when it comes to the evaluation of food or beverages.

- This sense covers the important factors of vibration; rough, smooth, sparkling; texture; viscosity or body; temperature; cold, warm, hot; hot as in peppery, alcoholic.

  We can quickly improve our evaluation skills if we learn to differentiate between the touch and taste senses, and then learn to verbalize these differences. Practice the words with the exercises.

- Remember, there are two palates, soft and hard, each with its own role. Be ever vigilant about registrations all over the mouth, including the lips, gums, teeth, roof of the mouth and throat area.

- Be alert to the significance of irritation to the eyes, nose and mouth.

- Nothing fools the wine judge more than temperature, cold or warm wine.

- Room temperature is ideal for red table wines, but room temperature is between 18–20°C (65–70°F), not a tent in the Sahara or an igloo in Iceland.

- Work hard at learning the difference between astringency and bitterness; also grape and wood tannins. Use the exercises provided.

WHAT DID YOU LEARN FROM THIS CHAPTER?

- Why is the *tactile* sense more important than the taste sense?
- Where in the mouth do we perceive the sense of touch?
- What are the main *tactile* sensations?
- Explain the difference between the *soft* and *hard* palate.
- Explain the difference between *astringency* and *bitterness.*
- What causes irritation?

CHAPTER 8

Any judging of wine can only be: by this group of people, from this bottle, at this place, at this time. No judgement can, possibly, be anything else.

—Alan Young, 1986

The greatest judge of them all—Bill Jamieson.

WINE JUDGING

It has taken this writer 30 years to realise that most wine competitions are either a hoax, a myth or entirely invalid; in some cases, absolutely fraudulent.

This in no way denigrates the efforts of thousands of people around the world who give up countless days and hours to running these charades. While people in various countries speak in awe of so-and-so who has a 'marvellous palate' (whatever that means), any judge can only be what she or he is. That person can not be anyone else, or see a wine any other way.

Why?

It is fair to ask why judging competitions are conducted anyhow? Most started as part of an agricultural show at the local municipal, shire or county fair, along with the best dressed clothes peg, best bull or ram, or maybe the best tray of lamingtons. The wine section gave three medals: gold for first, silver for second and a bronze for third just as did the children's' section for the best pencil drawing in the under seven years of age event.

The producers in the sections for cows, lambs and pumpkins etc., as well as wine producers, all learnt a lot from what was considered the best in any class through judges from near and far. In those times, there was only a blue ribbon for first place but nowadays to win an important event at one of these competitions can be worth a million dollars, regardless of how fraudulent the competition is.

Possibly the worst example of this is the Royal Melbourne Show in Australia, and the *Jimmy Watson Trophy* awarded to the best one-year-old red wine. For some astounding reason, this has for the past 25 years, captured the imagination of the media and consequently the wine drinking public. Yet it is almost impossible that the eventual purchaser of this much-vaunted wine can ever receive the same wine that won this award.

Raises questions

Firstly, being an event for one-year-old red wines, it is rarely possible that the wine will be in bottle at the time of the judging. More than likely, the Show entry wine came from one or two of the best barrels in the cellar; what the purchaser receives is a blend of all the barrels.

This is a worthwhile exposure of individual frailty, even though it affects the purchases of millions of wine lovers.

If you are the average wine buyer, influential wine writers who are often judges in some of these competitions, possibly guide you. Of course, they are going to defend their decisions and tout-up the wines that won at these competitions.

Are wine judges out of sync with the consumers - or are they merely another group of human beings expressing their preferences?

Wine Angels

A Nevada consulting group "Wine Angels" has analysed 30,000 wine reviews to reveal key flavour and aroma preferences for three of the USA's most read wine scribes. These writers influence millions of wine lovers the world over. A is an independent wine writer, B and C are writers for a high profile consumer mothly magazine.

The *Wine Marketer's Companion* analysed reviews of seven major wine varietals from the United States, Australia and New Zealand. Flavour and aroma attributes for Chardonnay, Cabernet Sauvignon, Merlot, Pinot noir, Sauvignon (blanc), Shiraz/Syrah, and Zinfandel are identified by reviewer and listed by frequency of occurrence in both 90 to 100 point reviews and all reviews. Also included are the associated average scores for each flavour/aroma attribute.

Pear fragrance

Big and small differences between the reviewers are revealed in the analysis. For example, pear is the most common attribute in the Chardonnay reviews by B and C; it occurs in 86 percent of B's and in 72 percent of C's 90- to 100-point reviews. On the other hand, pear shows up in only five percent of A's high-scoring Chardonnay reviews. As mentioned in earlier paragraphs, we all perceive the same stimulus in a different way and strength.

It should be pointed out that the pear aroma is most likely to come only from fruit grown in cool to cold climates which, in most cases, necessitates malo-lactic fermentations to soften the acids, thus confirming B and C's love of cool climate wines.

Hazelnuts

An example of where the reviewers do seem to be in agreement is in their mutual admiration of Chardonnays with hazelnut attributes. The average score for Chardonnay reviews that mention hazelnut is 90.8 points for both A and B. For C, Chardonnays with a hazelnut characteristic averaged 89.6 points; the choices of these three are only separated by 1.2%.

The flavour of hazelnuts is diacetyl (dimethyl diketone), produced during malo-lactic fermentation (MLF) so they all liked that flavour. You can purchase diacetyl at your local supermarket as imitation butter. So wines not undergoing MLF don't stand a chance with these reviewers. Is this a totally unbiased viewpoint?

Judges preferences

'Every reviewer seems to have unique flavour and aroma preferences. Knowing those preferences when making or marketing a wine could provide a competitive advantage in the marketplace,' said the reviewers. The same could be said for all wine competition judges.

Cullen's winery in Margaret River, Western Australia has for many years conducted a major Chardonnay event which attracts people and wine from around the world; no expense is spared. It is probably the world's premier Chardonnay judging as the results are divided into both Consumer and Industry categories.

Despite the fact that some of the Margaret River wines are among the world's best Chardonnays, these types of events do tend to favour local wines, regardless of whether the event is run in Argentina or Canada.

Where are the French?

So it was not surprising that local wines grabbed the top spots while California wines finished 5th, 7th, 10th, 14th and 16th. This was a far better result than the six Grand and Premier crus French wines from Chablis and the fabled Cotes d'Or. The Chablis wines finished in a quinella 19th, 20th and 21st places while the prohibitively expensive Cotes d'Or wines occupied 15th, 18th and 22nd places. So, what does this say about judging?

Let us have a quick look at another Australian consumer-industry judging, this one a superb black-tie event rather than an elegant down-on-the-farm show. The Hyatt Hotel in Adelaide, South Australia (SA) sponsors the annual SA Wine Competition for SA wines only.

There are 14 classes in all; from sparkling to dessert wines. I have watched this event from its inception as they copied my original concept of Australian wine judging from a decade previously, by having both male and female panels as well as industry and consumer judges. In my previous events consumers and industry judges agreed on the best wines only five percent of the time. That is to say, consumers and professionals disagreed 95% of the time!

In the beginning, the South Australians increased the difference between the consumers and judges to seven percent of the time, yet in 2002 they broke an all-time record with 100% disagreement. In the 14 classes there was not one agreement on the winning wines.

Lack of agreement

In conclusion, one could ask who is the world's best wine judge for you? Go to the nearest mirror and reflected in that adorable piece of glass you will see—the best judge of all.

There are many reasons why wine is judged—and each reason has a different method. For instance, the German and many French appellation systems require a simple judgment—pass or fail—no scoring necessary. This judgment is usually based on what is known as *typicity*; is the wine typical of the region or style. Many supermarket chain buyers also use this yes/no method as to whether a wine fits its price and quality requirements.

Wine competitions are more demanding. In Australian competitions the judges normally evaluate and score each wine individually and make comments about their perceptions of most wines. In general, US competitions do not point every wine, the wine is either of medal standard or dismissed. As the wines might come from many regions or even countries, this is very much in conflict with the typicity concept and it becomes more hedonistic—I like/dislike it.

Judging methods

When evaluating wine, one must ask the philosophical question, 'What are we judging?' Is it the best wine, does it fit our requirements—a hotel or restaurant will have different needs for banqueting (weddings and dinners) other than wine needed for the fine dining rooms. Does the wine meet regional typicity style, is it value-for-money, even the hedonistic I like it/I don't like it; there are many types of judgements.

As mentioned earlier, I like to divide wine into two categories—drinking or talking wines. Drinking wines are those uncomplicated products we purchase today, and drink today or tomorrow without any pretense or thought, even though a lot of this $5–10 style may well appear alongside $50–100 wines.

Talking wines are a little more serious. As King Edward VII is quoted as saying, 'Not only does one drink wine, but one inhales it, looks at it, tastes it, and then talks about it.' They are wines that we hold in our cellar and bring forth on a special occasion.

King Edward quote

Nevertheless, read this from Frank Prial, wine writer for *The New York Times* and long-time show judge, summing up the 2001 San Francisco International Wine Competition which attracted 2,783 wines from 16 countries and 22 of the United States: *If nothing else, the results of the competition would seem to show that, shorn of their carefully constructed mystiques, their beautiful labels and clever marketing, many expensive wines are not really that much superior to the less-expensive rivals. Maybe the veritas is in the vino.*

Best of Show white wine in the above competition was Giesen Marlborough (NZ) Sauvignon (blanc) retailing in the USA at $US11 which swept the board against all comers, many costing up to $100, and even more! In the eight varietal wine classes four wines costing $10 or less won four of the classes. Three standouts included a $5 Montepulciano d'Abbruzzi, and two $8 Australian wines from a then new label, Stonehaven.

This upstart producer took both the Syrah and Merlot classes against wines costing megabucks. Merlot, in particular, is a much revered and expensive wine in the two Northern California valleys—and other places.

Here the judge will be able to see the vintage and regional variations that will contribute largely to the *structure* and *body* (the bones and flesh) of the wine. Cooler climates in average seasons will provide optimal fruit for Chardonnay; not so in a cold or wet year. Inland, irrigated fruit in a hot year will provide very ordinary fruit but the same regions in a cool year will provide excellent fruit. It all depends on the weather—the right amounts of sunshine and rainfall—at the right times.

Following the judge's evaluation of what raw material the oenologist had to work with, the next question is what did he/she do with the fruit during processing?

Some wine media, and even judges, have an apparent love affair with oak flavour and the oak contribution to perceived quality. My understanding of what I have read in the wine press, and lots of judging experiences in many countries, makes me believe that a high level of heavily-toasted oak is acceptable in both red and white wines. I say no. To me anyhow, this is like listening to a symphony orchestra when the overbearing sound is continually that of the percussion section.

So many potentially very good wines judged recently were devastated by excessive heavily toasted oak, wines that should bomb-out in most competitions. Often I look back at my notes and repeatedly see 'too much heavy toasted oak.'

The myth of the 100-point wine judging scale

At least 10 years before Robert Parker thankfully abandoned a law practice in favour of wine writing, the 100-point scoring method was in vogue and practice, in and around the city of Melbourne, Australia. It had been copied from an Italian source.

After about a decade of use in the 1970s the system was abandoned and the 20-point system re-introduced by the group of trade professionals and writers who had dabbled with it. Their reasoning was that it was too "iffy"—what

Office International Wines & Vines (O.I.V.) Paris - score sheet

		Excellent	Very Good	Good	Unsatisfactory	To Eliminate	REMARKS
SIGHT	Appearance						
	Sparkling						
SMELL	Intensity						
	Quality						
TASTE	Intensity						
	Quality						
HARMONY							

Commonly used European score sheet - no numbers used, just ticks which really is scoring, but, by another method.

Two different score sheets

INTERNATIONAL WINE ACADEMY

HEDONIC SCORE SHEET   Date_____

WINE#.	Superb	Like very much		Like	OK		Not very good		Dislike		Bad		Food pairing
	20	19	18	17	16	15	14	13	12	11	10	9	8	7	6	5–0	

IN-MOUTH FLAVOR   PROFILES

Wine One   Two   Three   Four   Five   Six

WINE EVALUATION RECORD©

Name:_____ Place:_____ Date:_____

Blank WER

WINE DETAILS		SIGHT 4MAX	AROMA/ BOUQUET 6MAX	IN MOUTH 6MAX	AFTER-FLAVOR 2MAX	OVERALL 2MAX	TOTAL 20MAX	FOOD PAIRING
1	Vintage: Maker: Price: Variety: Region/Country:							
2	Vintage: Maker: Price: Variety: Region/Country:							
3	Vintage: Maker: Price: Variety: Region/Country:							
4	Vintage: Maker: Price: Variety: Region/Country:							
5	Vintage: Maker: Price: Variety: Region/Country:							
6	Vintage: Maker: Price: Variety: Region/Country:							

PRIOR TO IN-MOUTH
1. SIGHT
Appearance: Brilliant, star bright, bright, clear, dull, cloudy, precipitated.
Colour: Colourless, very light/light straw/straw green, light/medium/dark gold, pink, rose, light/purplish/medium/dark/tawny/brick red.
Saturation: Light/medium/deep.
Bubbles: Spritzig, size, quantity, rate, duration.

2. OLFACTORY
Aroma: Fruity, floral, spicy, vegetative, earthy.
Intensity: 1, 2, 3, 4, 5, 6, 7, 8, 9, 10.
Bouquet: Clean, fresh, dirty, H₂S (mercaptans), yeast, oak, SO₂ (no irritation).
Intensity: -5, -4, -3, -2, -1, 0, 1, 2, 3, 4, 5.

IN-MOUTH
3. OLFACTORY
Viscosity: Watery, thin, medium, full-bodied.
Taste: Sugar, bitter, sour, salt.
Olfactory/flavour: Earthy, fruity, floral, herbaceous, woody, sweet, complex.
Tactile: Temperature, texture, irritation, gas, viscosity.

• Bronze medal: 15.5 - 16.9   • Silver medal 17.0 - 18.4   • Gold medal 18.5 - 20.0

IN-MOUTH FLAVOR PROFILES

Above: A Wine Evaluation Record (WER) sheet *for you to copy.*

Below: A completed Wine Evaluation Record—*minus the food pairing.*

Completed WER

WINE DETAILS		SIGHT 4 max	AROMA/ BOUQUET 6 max	IN MOUTH 6 max	AFTER FLAVOUR 2 max	OVERALL 2 max	TOTAL 20 max
1	Vintage '01 Cullen Variety Chardonnay Region Margaret River WA	4	5,25	5,50	2	1,75	18,50
	Comments *Light gold colour–brilliant appearance, barrel-fermented, big on aromas of stone fruits and a little citrus. In-mouth the oaky flavours merge well with the good fruit. Stunning length and excellent finish*						
2	Vintage 01 Bouchard Pere Variety Chardonnay Region Le Montrachet	3,5	4,75	4,75	1,75	1,50	16,25
	Comments *Light straw colour–bright appearance, some melon & fig aromas, no apparent oak, medium after-flavour, bit short on complexity. Clean finish – just a little bitter.*						
3	Vintage 01 Robert Mondavi Variety Chardonnay Region Napa CA	3,75	5,25	5,25	1,75	1,75	17,75
	Comments *Medium straw colour–brilliant appearance; bold style with some pear, tropical fruit & mineral aromas; citrus, melon and butterscotch aromas - good oak balance. Crisp and excellent finish*						
4	Vintage 01 Hamilton-Russel Variety Chardonnay Region Walker Bay, S.Af	4	5,25	5,25	1,75	1,75	18
	Comments *Light golden colour–appearance star-bright. Definitive citrus–pear–green apple, cold climate aromas. Tons of fruit, supported by MLF butteriness. A smart wine——long after-flavour, drink now or better in 4-5 years.*						
5	Vintage 01 Floating Mtn Variety Chardonnay Region Waipara NZ	4	5,50	5,50	2	1,75	18,75
	Comments *Golden colour–appearance star bright, a wine with great promise, complex tropical fruits on nose - oak well balanced; has bracing, fresh mouth-feel and good length.*						

was the difference between an 89 and a 91. Well, the reasoning here was that the 91 wine was only one-fiftieth better than the 89 but commanded at least a 30% price premium. And on the 20 point scale a 91 point wine was only a silver medal—not even gold class.

The UC Davis 20 point system , has stepping-stones allocating the 20 points whereas the Italian 100 point system, despite being a five times 20-point count, is blurred about what you do with the 100 points. It included such vague items as finesse, harmony and fidelity to style.

System abandoned

It was also found that most people scored in the range of 65-85 points so why have a 100 points when you did nothing with the other 80 points. In early 2004, the World Wide Web produced another guide to allocating the 100 points. Unbelievably, only 10 points are allocated to *appearance* which I assume includes colour. The 'nose' receives up to 30 points, structure a weighty 20 points or one fifth of the total, finish 20 points and typicity 20 points. Little wonder that we see such awkward and worthless ratings.

The 100 point system has enormous appeal among the magazine fraternity—somehow or other it sells wine but thinking people around the world find it a bit of a laugh. One California lawyer suggests that 'really, the 100 point system could be consumer fraud if anybody ever wanted to push the issue with the Food and Drug Authority or consumer groups.'

Consumer fraud?

There is an ethical side to the 100 point system when used mainly by magazines as mentioned above. One thing for sure, in local competitions you can be assured that none of the judges know what the wines are. But is there any proof, not yet shown, that the media judgings are as scrupulous as the non-commercial events? One US magazine (*Wine Enthusiast*) has its ratings done by an outside organization which augers well for its authenticity.

What is the difference between an 87 and 91 points wine—many would ask if that difference would be there if the same wines were re-judged by the same people tomorrow? Rather than the fickleness of the 100 point system, why not just gold, silver and bronze ratings and then an 87 would be a silver medal just the same as a 91.

For convenience, bronze would be rated between 77–84 points, silver 85–92 and gold 93–100 points.

What next?

Well, it is easy to criticize other people's work; what about a constructive approach?

Ask any judge what are the main points that should be covered in wine judging? It would be interesting to hear the answers. Wine has, literally, evolved enormously in the past five decades but wine judging has stood still in this time and no-one seems comfortable with change. As one example, umami has come into the taste and flavour of wine but no one considers it as a factor in judging. It should be included equally among the 13 most important factors outlined below; factors that all wine judges should consider.

However, while something like 3,000 wines, give or take a few hundred or thousands, are accepted in major competitions, how can this enormous number of wines be given the time for fair judgement that the entry fees justify? After all, the average cost for entering one wine in a competition is rarely less than $US50 and more like $100 per entry, just imagine the cost for those entering 6 to 10 wines in each competition. Don't these people deserve a fair shake even though many of them are there purely for the medals rather than the judges' comments on how to improve their products?

The section on *sight*, that includes colour and appearance, is painfully misunderstood and rarely are conditions, such as correct lighting, suitable for worthwhile judgement of sight—*colour* and *appearance*. Whereas at our IWA judgements sight is accorded 20 percent of the overall score, it rarely is given 15 percent. So few judges understand this important aspect of judging so it is blissfully ignored.

Smell, as a well understood factor, is normally given its due worth while *taste* is totally misunderstood and given far more recognition than it deserves. As it is so often confused with *flavour*, it is doubted that many wine judges could describe what taste really implies. Much the same applies to *touch*, totally misunderstood and its value in wine mainly under-rated.

Again, *flavour* is confused with taste and rarely seen as its own person. *Concentration* is a much-discussed word, yet rarely does it appear on judge's comments whereas it should be on everyone. *Oak* is an issue that inflames the passion of many, yet it is not seen as an identity on its own

Some ignore *balance* and/or harmony, yet they are basic issues to others. It is difficult to make a judgement of wine without including balance, which most people would consider a basic issue. Of all these important issues, *length* is arguably what makes the difference between a good and an excellent wine.

Finish is what your mouth feels like when the wine has gone; is it 20 cents or a thousand bucks? Are you ready for the next course with a clean mouth without the leftover flavours of the last course? And, do you have the *after-flavour* (the memory) of the last wine? An abundance of length, finish and after-flavour are the facets that determine a great wine.

To implement this totally new type of scoring or judgement, wine competitions will have to scale-back the number of entries or renew their thinking on what wine judging is all about. At least three to five minutes will have to be allowed for the judgement of each wine. It is reasonable in some quarters to allow 20 wines per hour with refresher breaks at regular intervals

There are far too many entries in major shows, while national wine shows should be restricted to winners of regional/state wine shows—and not be run for the purpose of medal collections. Maybe wine competitions will have to review the medal count and present only first, second and third awards. This philosophy is starting to gather momentum among thinking people in the USA.

Main judging points

A NEW AND DIFFERENT JUDGING SHEET

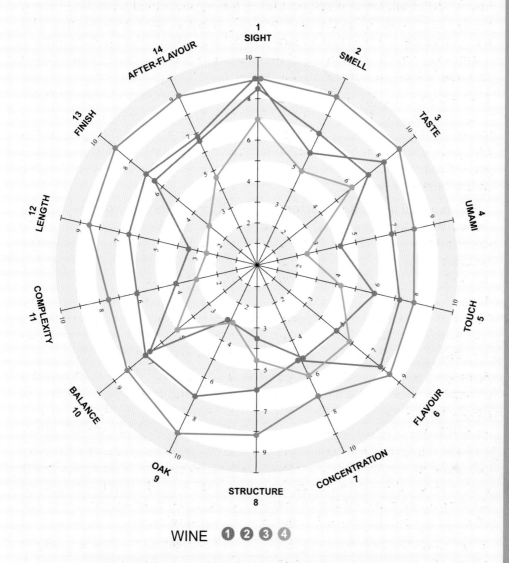

WINE ❶ ❷ ❸ ❹

RELATIVE VALUES OF WINE COMPONENTS

1. When judging wine it is most important that each and every wine is accorded the same total judging experience. To ensure this, over the years I have developed a number of fail-proof charts; this is the most recent.

2. Having progressively used the smell, the taste and touch vector wheels, you are now ready to put all this information together. To do that, you will find this Relative Values chart very useful. It is a visual view of what has happened in your mouth and brain.

3. On this wheel there are four wines being judged in the same class thereby showing their relative values, or why these hypothetical wines are different - or better.

4. The orange wine #4 is a bit wobbly, pretty much up-and-down around the circle, while the green wine #3 is a big wine in every respect.

5. Refer to the In-Mouth profiles on your Wine Evaluation Record chart for taste information and your Touch Record charts to help you complete the above Relative Values chart. Also utilise the Descriptive Analysis information to complete the smell vector.

MACEDON REGION PINOT NOIR PROFILE

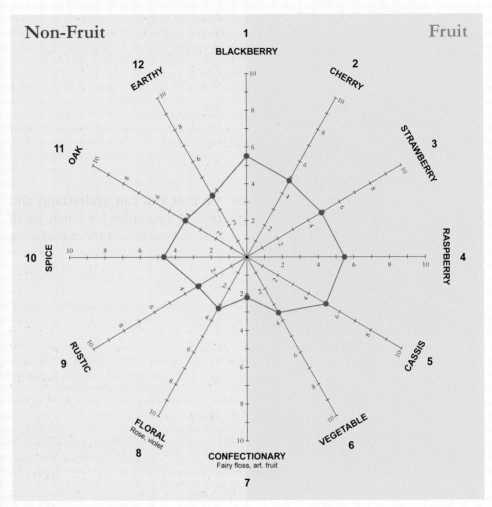

This 12 point vector is a compilation of averages by 12 people from my local Pinot noir study group to determine the regional flavours of our Macedon region Pinots noir.

The wines were in their youth, just 2–3 years old.

The chart shows a dominance of berry fruits and cherry flavours with a solid touch of spice—and much less vegetable and other non-fruit flavours. Confectionary refers to 'boiled lollies'.

During a 2004 student study tour in France, most of the wines evaluated were on the opposite—or non-fruit side of the vector, showing regional (typicity) rather than varietal character. Going on to Spain, there was a much stronger desire for fruity and varietal flavours.

DESCRIPTIVE ANALYSIS

The aim of this book has been to stress the individuality of wine and food lovers, and encourage them not to follow the pack. Each person seeks different flavours and has individual sensory perceptions. Competition judges seek winners of the various classes or categories and, as a rule, arrive at what they consider worthwhile judgements, regardless of where, when or how these judgements were made.

Aside from these competitions, the wine lover should seek wines he or she personally prefers and should not be influenced by competition results; events that were staged at another place at another time, from another bottle, by another group of people.

This book has provided many exercises so that you can understand and measure your personal sensory perceptions and thresholds for touch, smell and taste. You should now be able to recognise the many components of wine you like or dislike, and be able to quantify these hedonic pleasures. Having gained this knowledge, you will be able to make positive and qualified choices of preferred wines. Hence, your main purpose in evaluating wines will be to select your preferred wines.

In my sensory evaluation seminars I endeavor to teach, not which wine is best—and best has to be qualified and a subject of personal interest only, but rather how four similar wines, from the same grape variety, are different. These wines can be four Chardonnays, Pinots noir, Rieslings, Tempranillo, Zinfandels or any other variety. They may all come from the same district or four different countries; but why are they different?

My sensory evaluation seminars conclude with the following descriptive analysis and in-mouth profiling exercise. These will bring you to 'concert pitch.' Do not think that doing this on one occasion will be any great salvation; it won't. But it will open the door to a new experience, a truly professional experience. I have participated in these exercises many thousands of times and still learn much on every occasion. Remember that training our senses is similar to training our muscles and mind—practise makes perfect.

These exercises were introduced to me by Dr A.C. Noble, so I will let her explain what they are all about. Her article appeared in the *American Wine Society Journal*:

The big difference between descriptive analysis and quality rating lies in the objective, analytical, specific terminology employed in the former approach versus the hedonic, evaluative and judgemental assessment of the latter. The primary problem which arises in the use of quality scorecards is that it is a judgement based on overall perception. Since quality is a composite response to the sensory properties of the wine, based on our expectations which have developed from our previous experiences with a wide range of wines and our own personal preferences, this judgement is an individual response. No two people integrate the individual attributes in the same way, much less have the same preferences.

Two simple examples can illustrate this. Presented with a generic Californian red wine with 1–2 per cent sugar and a dry Cabernet Sauvignon, most wine drinkers claim to prefer the latter (although an enormous market exists for the former wine type). Using expert judges to rate the quality of these two wines may result in their being scored 12 and 17 on the Davis 20 point scorecard, but only by a more descriptive approach can the wines be meaningfully differentiated. One has to know the preferences of the judges to even guess which wine was given the 17.

In the second example, when presented with 10 Chardonnays and asked to pick the higher quality wine, five experts chose wine A and five chose wine B. The conclusion is not that the wines are not different, but that the experts had different quality assessments and preferences. By a descriptive approach, we learn that wine A has an intense oak aroma and very little fruit, whereas wine B is characterised by apricot, apple and honey notes, with some vanilla.

The major requirements for terms used in descriptive evaluation of wine is that the terms be specific and capable of being defined. Clearly, subjective hedonic nomenclature does not meet this criterion, since such terms usually have a different meaning to each individual. Apricot, vanilla and black pepper are specific terms which can be defined unequivocally with physical standards. In contrast, rich; good nose, vinous; middle-roundness, high nality are vague and imprecise adjectives, which cannot be understood by others without extensive discussion, if at all.

While this exercise can be performed solo, it is quite easy to set up for five, 10 or 20 people as it is for one. You can try the exercise with 8–10 standards or modify it to have only 3–4 standards.

In our classes we use an eight point vector while in our professional events we use 12–16 standards—depending on the complexity of the wine. See illustration on page s 156, 161 and 165.

For the 8 point profile we need a jug, flagon or cask commercial red/white wine, preferably bland (for the standards) and an eye dropper.

Pour 30–45ml or one to one and a half ounces into each of 10 glasses. Mark the foot of each glass with a felt pen with C or the number of the sample, the first and last glass in the lineup is marked with C to indicate 'control' wine. Number the remaining glasses 1 through 8.

For white wine evaluation	For red wine evaluation
Glass W1 Lemon	Glass R1 Cherry
Glass W2 Apple	Glass R2 Plum
Glass W3 Melon	Glass R3 Strawberry
Glass W4 Pineapple	Glass R4 Cassis (black currant)
Glass W5 Pear	Glass R5 Raisin
Glass W6 Apricot	Glass R6 Black Pepper
Glass W7 Floral	Glass R7 Vanilla
Glass W8 Diacetyl (imitation butter)	Glass R8 Soy/Vegemite

Procedure

Prepare the standards and set them in the center of the table (see page 162).

Each judge has 4–6 wines to be evaluated in the glasses in front of them, and each judge will require an eight point vector sheet with sufficient points to cover the number of standards. Each of the standards glasses should be covered with a numbered petrie dish lid, saucer or other suitable cover, so that the room doesn't smell like a perfume factory, nor the judges become confused by the accumulation of smells.

Prior to smelling any glass, the lid should be held firmly on the glass, then the glass rotated or shaken. The glass should be taken to the nose before removing the lid otherwise a lot of the odor will dissipate.

Each person should smell the control wine to commence the exercise, then smell any numbered standard. Having memorised this component, the judge then smells the wines to be evaluated to determine, on a scale of 10, how much of that particular component is in the four wines, and then marks this intensity with an X on that particular 'spoke'.

So, if your first standard is R2, you would mark the 'cherry' spoke with an X representing the intensity you gauged for each wine. You should mark the intensity with the number of the wine judged, numbering 1–4 from the left. (See Fig B below).

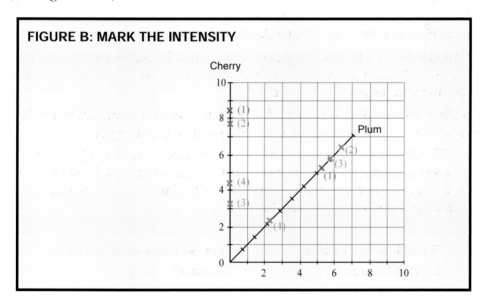

FIGURE B: MARK THE INTENSITY

Philosophy repeat

Now, smell the control wine again (do this before you smell each standard) and try another standard, this time maybe the next one will be Rl, ethyl acetate. Repeat the above procedure, marking the intensity of ethyl acetate in each of your four wines. Next, join up the two spokes with colored pencils or coded lines (see Fig C next page).

Differences between systems

**Actual
differences**

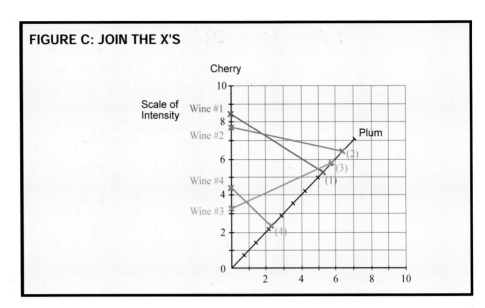

FIGURE C: JOIN THE X'S

Scale 10 of Intensity—0 in the centre —10 highest (outside)

Wine 1_____ Wine 2 .... Wine 3 ------------ Wine 4 - • - • - • -

Figure C: Mark your color or line code at the bottom of your sheet.

Proceed to measure the intensity of each of the standards, remembering to:

1. Smell the control wine before each standard.

2. Swirl each glass with the lid held firmly on until you bring the glass to your nose.

Early in your smelling career this exercise will quickly fatigue your olfactory receptors. Should you suffer smell fatigue, smell a glass of water and, if necessary, leave the room and go for a walk. When evaluating your four wines, close your eyes. while smelling—it helps if you concentrate.

Let's try to put it all together on an eight point profile with four Merlots from one region and find out how they are different.

This eight point profile, opposite, tells us that:

Wine No. 1 had significant amounts of cherry, plum, cassis, and oak. Low in strawberry, raspberry, licorice and tobacco.

Wine No. 2 Strong on red berry and stone fruits, was lower in cassis, licorice, tobacco and oak aromas.

Wine No. 3 Wines 3 had strong berry, cherry, strong raspberry, cassis and tobacco and plum. Wine 3 also had a lot of tobacco and strong oak.

Wine No. 4 had reasonable cherry and tobacco, cassis and licorice,   but low in oak.

8 Point MERLOT Vector

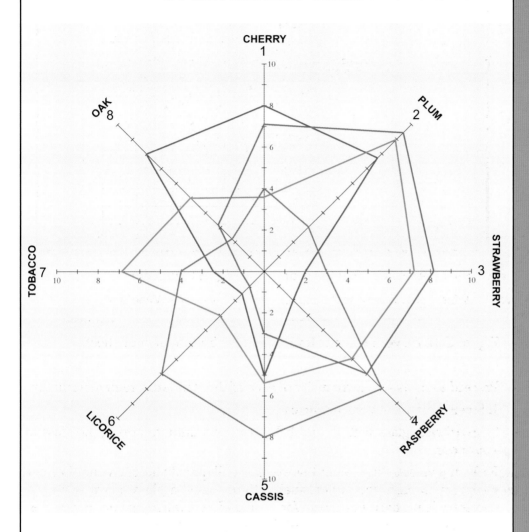

DESCRIPTIVE ANALYSIS RECORD

Spokes can have name change e.g.Floral could be changed to Oak. Any names can be added to the spokes for red or white wine discrimination.

1. **SMELL** the control wine
2. **SWIRL** the glass and smell the aroma of the first wine.
3. **RATE** the intensity of the first aroma attribute on a 1–10 scale.
    0 is none. 10 = high. Smell the wine as often as necessary—remembering olfactory fatigue.
4. **RATE** the intensity of the same attribute in the remaining wines in the order they are listed below.
5. **SMELL** the control wine after each sample
6. **EVALUATE** the remaining AROMA attributes in the wines **before** rating the flavour terms

Use either coloured pens or dots and dashes etc., for each wine

Wine 1 _____ Wine 2 .... Wine 3 ------------ Wine 4 - • - • - • -

DESCRIPTIVE ANALYSIS

TABLE SET-UP FOR 6 PERSONS

In front of each judge/taster are four wines which will be evaluated by descriptive analysis.

In the centre of the table are 10 glasses. A control wine (unadulterated) is located at each end.

All other numbered glasses are the same wine as the control—but have a standard added.

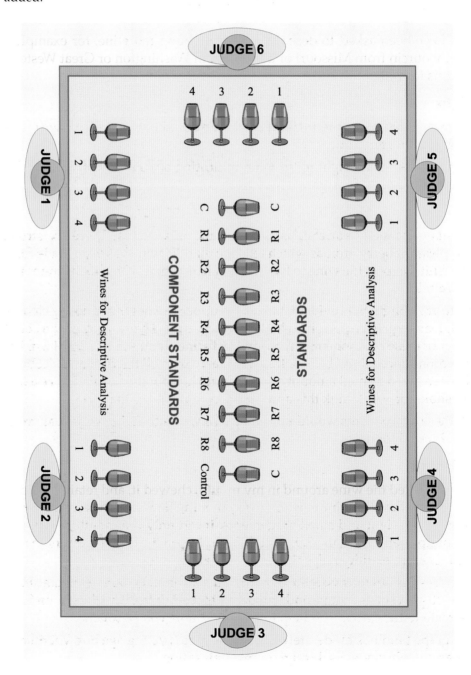

TELLING THE WORLD WHAT YOU THINK!

The time has come to put your words where your wine was.

If you have followed the summaries of each chapter, filled in your hedonic wine evaluation records and completed your descriptive analysis sheets, you are now equipped to stand up and speak about any wine in a totally objective and intelligent manner. But above all, in non-jargon, easily understood, descriptive terms.

Not only will you be articulate and cover every point, but you will be using words that are understood in Auckland NZ, Austin TX, Adelaide, London, Niagara Falls, Hong Kong, or Sacramento CA.

You have been asked to describe a typical young red wine, for example a Chambourcin from Missouri or a Syrah from Washington or Great Western. Try this formula:

Sight

Colour—intense deep red with the colour extending to the very edge of the tongue; no watery rim.

Appearance—star bright to brilliant, indicating a wine of high acidity. I've given it 3.75/4.00 for sight.

Speak with confidence

Smell

Aroma—Distinctly varietal, as I understand this variety. There are strong and pleasant berry aromas which tells me that the wine has been made from ripe fruit. I expect the wine to have a lot of fruit when I come to the in-mouth appraisal.

Bouquet—Slight SO_2, evident, tickles the upper reaches of the nose—alcohol is high enough to be perceived in the nasal passage. I have no objection about either of these components in a young red wine. To my threshold, the oak is also pronounced, but I believe this will marry with all the fruit and alcohol. I also perceived a small amount of volatile acidity, but then again I have a low threshold for VA. I think this adds to the complexity of the wine.

All these components would portend a lively, mouth-filling wine. I scored it at 5.25/6.00 for nose.

In-Mouth

Having rolled the wine around in my mouth, chewed it, and retained it long enough to allow the wine to warm in my mouth, the first impression confirms my external sight and smell judgements. It certainly is a mouthful of wine, lots of ripe berry fruit, the SO_2 is slightly drying on the roof of the mouth and the touch of volatility helps the smell appraisal.

Speak YOUR mind

Tactile—The obvious viscosity confirms the alcohol, I would estimate about 12½–13 per cent, the grape and wood tannins certainly fill up the mouth from the teeth to the throat, and help make this a more complex wine.

The grape tannin is moderately aggressive at this young age but will round-out as the wine evolves through bottle maturation.

SYRAH 12 POINT VECTOR

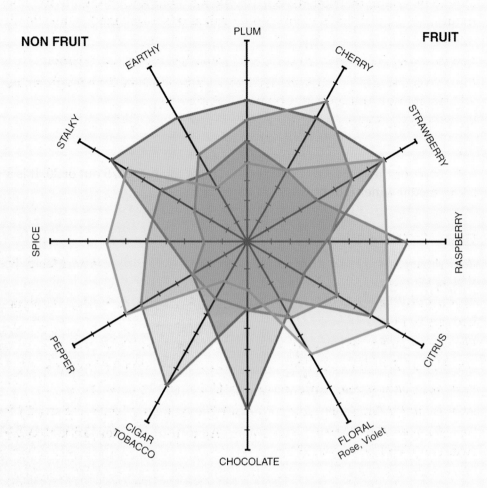

NON FRUIT   FRUIT

PLUM

EARTHY

CHERRY

STALKY

STRAWBERRY

SPICE

RASPBERRY

PEPPER

CITRUS

CIGAR
TOBACCO

FLORAL
Rose, Violet

CHOCOLATE

This vector illustrates how four people perceived the same wine. They may well have scored the wines all the same points, but here is a diagram of what they actually perceived.

Temperature—this wine has been served too warm and highlights the alcohol

The acidity that was obvious from the brilliant appearance is evident on the teeth and tongue. My personal opinion is this wine is a very good long-term cellaring wine, eight years plus. I also appreciate the slightly perceivable bitterness at the back of the mouth.

Being a young wine the acids and tannins are astringent and out of balance, but these along with the abundant berry fruit are what I think makes it such a good cellaring wine. Not ready to drink yet.

My score for the in-mouth evaluation 4.75/6.00.

Temperature—
very important

After-flavour

Due to its youth, the after-flavour is awkward, bits and pieces all over the mouth but is persistent showing good fruit and is a well made wine, in my opinion.

Length—certainly goes well back in the mouth showing its good points.

Finish—the acid certainly gives it a clean, acidic finish - a little rough on the edges right now but will develop in the bottle.

As it will continue to improve, I currently rate it at 1.75/2.00.

Overall

1.75 extra for the overall impression, making a total of 17.75 out of 20. It is a silver medal wine right now.

Do NOT forget these

BIBLIOGRAPHY

Basic Principles of Sensory Evaluation, American Society for Testing & Materials, Washington D.C.

Sensory Processes, Alpern, Lawrence and Wolsk Brooks/Cole, Michigan University Press

Flavor Texture Perception, C.M. Christensen, Academic Press

The Human Body, Brian R Ward, Franklin Watts, London & New York

Wine and Conversation, Adrienne Lehrer, University Indiana Press

Wine is Fun!, Alan Young, International Wine Academy, San Francisco, 1995

Chardonnay: Your International Guide, Alan Young, International Wine Academy, San Francisco, 1994

INDEX

The Wine Appreciation Guild has been an educational pioneer in our fascinating community. —Robert Mondavi

Your opinion matters to us...

You may not think it, but customer input is important to the ultimate quality of any revised work or second edition. We invite and appreciate any comments you may have. And by registering your WAG books and other information products you are enrolled to receive prepublication discounts, special offers, or alerts to various wine events, only available to registered members.

REGISTRATION FORM

Name_____Date_____

Professional Affiliation_____

Address_____

_____

City_____State_____Zip_____

e-mail_____

What book or other product did you purchase?_____

How did you discover this book (or other product?_____

_____

Was this book required class reading? Y N

School/Organization_____

Where did you acquire this book?_____

Was it a good read? (circle)   Poor 1 2 3 Excellent

Was it useful to your work? (circle)   Poor 1 2 3 Excellent

Suggestions_____

_____

_____

Comments_____

_____

_____

You can register your book by phone: (800) 231-9463; Fax: (650) 866-3513; e-mail: Info@WineAppreciation.com; or snail mail (copy and send to: Product Registration, Wine Appreciation Guild, 360 Swift Avenue, South San Francisco, CA 94080).